Books ar

Computer-aided Draughting Workbook

City and Guilds Co-publishing Series

City and Guilds of London Institute has a long history of providing assessments and certification to those who have undertaken education and training in a wide variety of technical subjects or occupational areas. Its business is essentially to provide an assurance that pre-determined standards have been met. That activity has grown in importance over the past few years as government and national bodies strive to create the right conditions for the steady growth of a skilled and flexible workforce.

Both teachers and learners need materials to support them as they work towards the attainment of qualifications, and City and Guilds is pleased to be working with several distinguished publishers towards meeting that need. It has been closely involved in planning, author selection and text appraisal, although the opinions expressed in the publications are those of the individual authors and are not necessarily those of the Institute.

City and Guilds is fully committed to the projects listed below and is pleased to commend them to teaching staff, students and their advisers.

Carolyn Andrew and others, *Business Administration Level I* and *Business Administration Level II*, John Murray
David Minton, *Teaching Skills in Further and Adult Education*, Macmillan
Graham Morris and Lesley Reveler, *Retail Certificate Workbook* (Levels 1 and 2), Macmillan
Peter Riley (consultant editor), *Computer-aided Engineering*, Macmillan
Barbara Wilson, *Information Technology: the Basics*, Macmillan
Caroline Wilkinson, *Information Technology in the Office*, Macmillan

Computer-aided Draughting Workbook

Brian J. Townsend

Project Manager
Havering College of Further and Higher Education
Hornchurch

Consultant Editor: Peter Riley
Head of Department of Engineering Technology
Blackpool and The Fylde College

MACMILLAN

City and Guilds

First published 1993 by
THE MACMILLAN PRESS LTD
Houndmills, Basingstoke, Hampshire RG21 2XS
and London
Companies and representatives
throughout the world

ISBN 0–333–56504–5

A catalogue record for this book is
available from the British Library.

Printed in Hong Kong

10 9 8 7 6 5 4 3 2 1
01 00 99 98 97 96 95 94 93

Acknowledgements

Thanks are due to Briamar Design Services for permission to use Figure 1.2.

Both my parents died during the writing of this book –
it is dedicated to their memory

Contents

Introduction

The availability of sophisticated, low-cost computer-aided draughting, or CAD, systems means that they are being used by an increasing number of organisations. The savings in labour costs and the increases in productivity that result from the efficient use of CAD are one side of the coin. The other side includes the broadening of career prospects in the field of design, particularly for those coming from a traditional draughting background.

This workbook aims to give practical knowledge about how CAD can be used for draughting and design. It follows closely the requirements of the City and Guilds Computer-aided Engineering 230 series. It will also be appropriate for those studying other equivalent courses, such as those offered by the Business and Technology Education Council (BTEC).

Traditional draughting tasks become simpler and faster when full advantage is taken of CAD. These aims will be more rapidly achieved if the CAD trainee puts the theory into practice. The learning assignments in this workbook provide just this practice. This 'hands-on' approach means that the trainee must have access to a commercial CAD system. If this is not possible at the trainee's place of work, a local college may be able to offer open-access CAD facilities.

A CAD system may be developed for use in a particular area of design. Different systems are likely to have different operating commands, system input and output methods, and so on. Any such differences are usually in name only and can easily be translated between systems.

Other aspects of CAD, such as the control of manufacturing processes by computer and the advantages of using CAD in a manufacturing context, are dealt with in other books in the City and Guilds/Macmillan publishing for computer-aided engineering. Details are given below.

Because of rapid technological advances this is an exciting time to be involved in CAD. This workbook has been written for those concerned with sharing and exploiting the benefits that may be derived from these advances.

City and Guilds/Macmillan publishing for computer-aided engineering

This workbook is one of a series of City and Guilds/Macmillan books which together give complete and up-to-date coverage of computer-aided engineering. A core text, or source book (*Computer-aided Engineering*), gives basic information on all the main topic areas (basic CNC; CNC setting and operation; CNC part programming; CNC advanced part programming; basic CAD/CAM; computer-aided draughting; advanced CAD; basic robotics; robot technology; programmable logic controllers; more advanced programmable logic controllers). It has tasks structured in to the text to encourage active learning.

Workbooks cover five main topics: CNC setting and operation; CNC part programming; computer-aided draughting; robot technology; programmable logic controllers. Each workbook includes all the operational information and guidance needed to be able to complete the practical assignments and tasks.

The books complement each other but can be used independently of each other. Peter Riley (Head of Department of Engineering Technology, Blackpool and The Fylde College) is Consultant Editor of the series.

How to use this book

Each learning assignment in this workbook has a similar structure, to make its use as straightforward as possible. Information and guidance that is needed to be able to complete the practical work is included with each assignment.

You will be able to identify the following parts of the text:

- Background information introducing the topic at the beginning of each assignment

- Other relevant knowledge given under the heading 'Additional information'.

- In the sections 'Useful observations' you will find points which will help you in becoming familiar with the process and in exploring ways in which it can be used.

- The practical 'Tasks' are presented in a logical sequence so that they can be accomplished safely and successfully. In many cases 'Additional tasks' are included to reinforce and enhance the basic practical work.

- If there is information of particular interest concerning the practical tasks, you will find this under the heading 'A point to note' or 'Points to note'.

All the diagrams and illustrations which are needed for each assignment are given at the appropriate point in the text.

You are recommended to obtain a folder in which to keep work which you have completed. This will serve as a record of your achievements and may be useful for future reference.

Operating procedures

A CAD system, because it is mains-powered, is potentially dangerous. You, as the user, are responsible for reporting any obvious signs of danger to yourself or to others. Figure 1.1 shows a basic checklist for any CAD system. Any equipment that fails the checklist must be corrected by a competent person before the system is used.

CAD system arrangements

A 'stand-alone' CAD system consists of a single computer system with appropriate input and output devices. Several CAD systems may be connected to a network so that software, drawing files and expensive output equipment can be shared. There are some operating differences with a networked system and access may involve the use of passwords.

Every CAD system will have the same basic units but there are differences in the type of input or output devices. A typical stand-alone system will use a personal computer (PC) with a colour display for visual output and a standard keyboard for input. For easier input of drawing instructions, a pointing device such as a mouse or a digitising tablet may be used. A plotter is often used for the production of a paper-based output.

> Mains supply sockets not damaged.
> Mains supply plugs not damaged.
> Mains supply cables not damaged.
> Unit casings in position and secure.
> No obvious damage to any system unit.
> Interconnecting cables not damaged.
> Interconnecting cables connected securely.
> No trailing cables that could be tripped over.

▲ **Figure 1.1** A basic system checklist

◀ **Figure 1.2** A typical stand-alone CAD system

Additional information

After you have gained access to the system, a 'menu' is usually presented on the display screen. The choice you are given depends on whether or not the computer system is used for activities other than CAD. A wordprocessor feature may be offered to allow the input of large amounts of text to a CAD design. Menus may be supplied either with the computer or with the CAD program. They may be bought or, like that shown in Figure 1.3, designed within the organisation.

USEFUL OBSERVATION

Figure 1.2 shows that the equipment has a fairly compact layout, so that you can avoid unnecessary stretching. Although personal preferences are important, you can avoid aches and pains if the system parts are arranged in a way that allows you to maintain a correct posture. A right-handed layout is shown, but this can be changed for left-handed users as neither the keyboard or the digitiser device is 'handed'.

```
****************************
* B R I A M A R   D E S I G N S *
*           ----O----           *
*   C O M P U T E R - A I D E D  *
*   D R A U G H T I N G   A N D  *
*     D E S I G N   O F F I C E  *
****************************

            M A I N   M E N U

      1. Park the Hard Disc
      2. Enter the CAD system
      3. Enter the Wordprocessor
      4. Enter the Database
      5. Enter the Root Directory
      6. Make a Backup Disc

Please enter the menu number and press ENTER

   In the event of a system problem, please
          inform the System Manager.
```

▶ **Figure 1.3** A typical user-designed menu

A POINT TO NOTE

The type of menu shown in Figure 1.3 does not provide password protection.

On leaving the CAD system, you will be returned to the Main Menu. If no more computer use is required, parking the hard disc may be the next choice. Some computer systems have automatic hard disc parking when the mains supply is removed.

This workbook cannot cover all the types of starting-up and closing-down procedures that exist for CAD systems. You should receive instructions from the 'system manager' when there is any doubt.

On completing the design activity, you need to close the CAD system down in a way that ensures the design is not lost. This may require the design to be 'saved' on external magnetic storage such as floppy disc or tape. A logging-off activity is usually required on CAD systems that have a password requirement.

TASKS

Task 1.1 Operating procedure

- Carry out the inspection of a CAD system using the checklist given in Figure 1.1. (Note: It is *neither desirable nor necessary* for a system to be deliberately made unsafe or faulty in any way before this assignment is carried out.)
- Execute the correct start-up procedure for your CAD system including, if necessary, the use of passwords for system access.
- Load and re-save an existing drawing. (No drawing activity is required for this task.)
- Execute the correct closing-down procedure for a CAD system, including the switching-off of all system units such as the computer and the printer.

Learning Assignment 2

Draughting parameters

In the creation of a drawing using pre-CAD methods, the draughtsperson will first decide on the size of paper to use. The appearance of the final drawing will then be a combination of the individual's draughting skills and the drawing standards in force within the organisation.

In a CAD system, the skills of the user include setting up the system, monitoring its performance and then making any required corrections to the initial settings. The aim is to make the CAD system operate in the most efficient way for the work in hand.

Whether or not an organisation uses CAD, it will usually have a basic policy that specifies certain standard features to be used on all drawings. These features may include line and text styles, borders, title blocks and so on. In a CAD system, these features are specified in a 'standard' or 'prototype' drawing. It may also include specifications for details such as arrowhead sizes, different colours for different line styles, layers for construction lines, hatched sections, dimensions, text, and so on.

Additional information

The standard drawing may include 'drawing aids' such as the capture of points on a grid, line ends, midpoints, automatic orthogonal line drawing and ruled axes. Different measuring systems are available to satisfy the varied uses of CAD systems: for example, an engineering organisation may specify dimensions in millimetres but an architectural designer is likely to use feet and inches. Different angular measurement systems and precision specifications are also usually provided.

A typical standard drawing for a CAD system would have the following minimum specification:

grid spacing – equal or unequal in x and y
drawing units and accuracy
point capture increments
drawing limits
layers
'paper' or non-paper screen (background colour).

USEFUL OBSERVATION

There is no 'best way' to produce a drawing. As you learn about your CAD system, you will develop a procedure that suits you best. Most CAD systems allow a wide variety of procedures to be used to achieve a given output.

TASKS

Task 2.1 Draughting parameters

Note No drawing activity is required for Task 2.1. It should be recognised that the identification of existing parameters on a standard drawing may only be achieved when the drawing is being created. Therefore, such data will be obtained in a later task.

- Establish the parameters of a standard blank drawing sheet, using the appropriate reference manuals and organisation documents, and fill in the Standard Drawing Sheet Checklist (Figure 2.1) as fully as possible.
- Make a brief subjective assessment of the reason(s) for the choice of parameters and complete the last part of the checklist.

►Figure 2.1

STANDARD DRAWING SHEET CHECKLIST			
Feature	Yes	Feature	Yes
Object and point capture		Grid points	
Ruler axes		Drawing limits	
Elevation setting		Thickness setting	
Entity colour		Co-ordinates display	
Alternative units for dimensions		Standard drawing sheet with company details	
Orthogonal drawing		Screen background colour	
Text size		Draw dynamically – drag	
Text styling		Multiple layers	
Tablet/mouse selection		Line type selection	
Screen menu/s		Pulldown/popup menus	
Time/date stamping		Dimension tolerance	
Subjective assessment of reason/s for choice of features			

A POINT TO NOTE

The list in Figure 2.1 is not meant to be exhaustive. Your CAD system may include features that have been omitted to avoid confusion at this introductory stage.

Learning Assignment 3

Software configuration

This Assignment deals with the input of user information to the CAD system so that it operates correctly during the design activity. For example, all the digitiser devices known as 'mice' or 'pucks' produce the same effect on the screen. There are marked differences between the devices, though: they may have two, three or four buttons and either a 'serial' or a 'bus' connection to the computer. Therefore, the CAD system software has to be set up so that it matches the digitiser device correctly.

The monitor(s) used on a CAD system will have been selected to satisfy a perceived requirement at an acceptable cost. If the maximum drawing area for a given screen size is required, the commands and/or menus will need to be displayed on a separate, low-resolution monitor. A large number of CAD systems use a monitor that displays the drawing, one screen menu and the last two or three commands simultaneously. The type of design work usually determines whether a high- or medium-resolution monitor is used.

From the above, you will have realised that all the input/output parts of a CAD system have features that need to be 'known' by, or aligned to, the CAD system software before the system can be used. This procedure is usually known as 'configuring'. The reference manual or installation guide for your CAD system will contain details of this procedure.

Additional information

Some CAD systems may be commanded to display the current configuration for the user to change or confirm it as required. Others may erase the current configuration and require all the data to be input again. In the latter case, a written record of the data must be kept to avoid the need to find someone in the organisation who remembers the previous configuration data.

TASKS

Task 3.1 Software configuration

In this task, you are asked to change the input device on your CAD system. It is suggested that a suitable device for these tasks would be a mouse that differs from the type that is normally used on the system.

- Connect the replacement device to the CAD system.
- Enter the CAD system and select the configuration option.
- Establish and record the configuration parameters for the original device.
- Use the device driver options presented by the system software to select that which suits the new device.
- Record the device parameters and leave the configuration facility.
- Test the newly configured CAD system with the new device. (This may mean that the system has to be restarted in order to initialise the software again.)

Learning Assignment 4

Creating standard drawing sheets

The basic drawing commands on any CAD system must include the creation of single lines, the creation of multi-lined figures or polygons, the creation of arcs and circles, the combining of all these features and the creation of text. The editing of the resulting features is also a requirement.

Fortunately, most CAD systems use the same names for these features. Thus, to draw a line, the command called LINE will be used; for an arc, the ARC command will be used. Text is usually produced by using the TEXT command, and all these commands will be entered at the keyboard or selected from a command menu using a mouse or puck.

Additional information

After using a MULTI-LINE or POLY-LINE command, subsequent editing features such as erasing, moving or copying will refer to the whole figure, not just to one line or element in that figure. This is one example of many CAD time-saving features.

Text is usually treated in the same way as a multi-line so that editing operations apply to the whole text entry. The 'Enter' or 'Return' key is used to signify the end of a line of text. It will also tell the CAD system that the use of that command has ended and so, in many CAD systems, each line of text is a separate entity.

Task 4.1 Starting a design

To obtain practice in using these simple commands, you are asked to try to create the design shown in Figure 4.1 – the actual shape and size of the final design is not important. Note that the crosses are construction aids that do not normally appear on the printed output – they can be turned on or off during the designing session.

The design is based on an A4 standard drawing sheet with a grid and point capture separation of 20 mm squares – these are indicated by crosses. If you cannot match this value, get as close as possible. Leave all the other features of the standard drawing, such as line style and layer, unchanged at this stage. Produce two versions of the design: one using the LINE command and the other using the MULTI-LINE command. Save both versions, using different names, for future tasks.

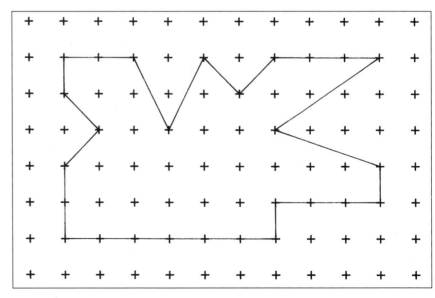

▶ **Figure 4.1** A simple drawing task

The actual creation and saving of the designs will use commands that apply to the CAD system you are using. You may need 'local' help before you can draw the design. At this stage, all you have to do is move the pointing device to the desired grid point, lock on to it and then press the Enter key or digitiser button; co-ordinate values are not required.

Task 4.2 Editing a design

In this task, you will learn about the different effects of the general ERASE command.

- Retrieve the design created with the LINE command from Figure 4.1 and select the ERASE command – this may have a different name on the system you are using.
- A line is identified by moving a small cursor symbol, such as a square or circle, over the line and pressing the digitiser button called the 'pick' button. Try out this feature. (Turn off the point capture mode first so that the cursor symbol does not lock on to the wrong entity.)
- Confirm the entity removal by pressing the Enter key or digitiser button. Try this now by erasing the indicated line on Figure 4.2. If you are successful, continue to remove the entities, one by one.
- Some CAD systems allow you to 'unerase', or restore, an entity that has been removed in error. Try this feature also.
- If you meet a problem in erasing, find out the reason before going on. The ability to edit a design with the ERASE facility is crucial to your efficient use of a CAD system.
- When you are confident about the selection and erasure of an entity, find and use any other single entity ERASE features that the CAD system offers.

ADDITIONAL TASK

Now retrieve your MULTI-LINE design and try to erase the line indicated on Figure 4.2. If your CAD system follows the normal rule, the whole design is selected – you may want this sometimes. If the design was created using a MULTI-LINE command and you *then* want to erase part of that design, a conversion into separate entities may be allowed. Again, you are not required to save this edited design but if you do, use a new name.

USEFUL OBSERVATION

A tolerance on the symbol position may be allowed by the system, which will respond to your choice in a particular way. A message in the command area, a flashing symbol on the entity or making the entity dotted are typical responses. If your selection is inaccurate, an indication should be given.

POINTS TO NOTE

You do *not* have to save your edited design. But if you do save it, use a different name from the original because the design with that name is to be used again.

As you will be saving several drawings as you work through the various tasks in this workbook, you should make a record of the names used, together with a brief description of each drawing, its task number and its creation date.

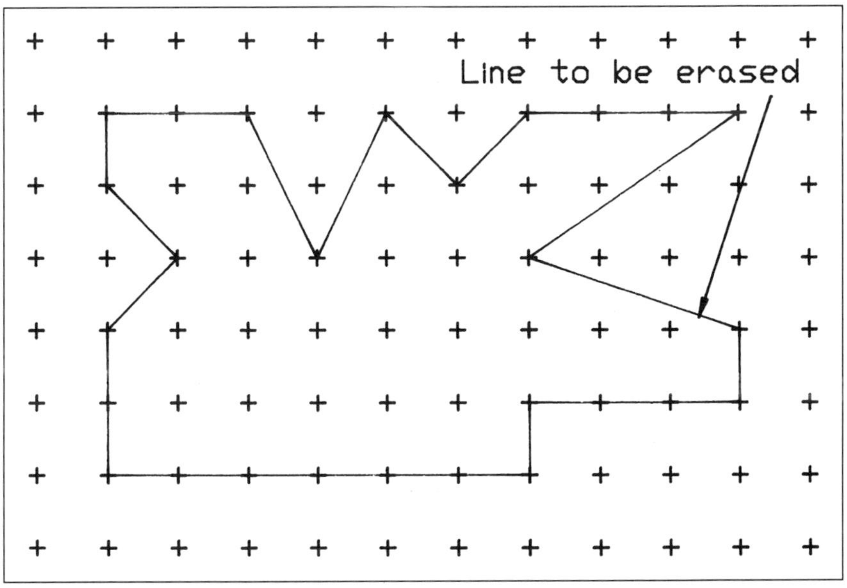

◀ **Figure 4.2** Erasing a line

9

Task 4.3 Adding text to a design

CAD systems allow users to input text in various sizes, styles, fonts, positions and orientations. An organisation normally specifies these parameters but a customer may want different text formats. This task gives practice in creating different text.

Text is obtained using the command TEXT or similar. The response is a series of prompts. These require user input about the text position, its size and its angle. Parameters relating to style, font and so forth are input as a separate exercise if the standard settings have to be changed. This procedure has many variations, so you must find out what method is used on your system and then use its values.

- Several text sizes, positions and angles are shown on Figure 4.3; try to modify your multi-line design to match the figure. An identical result is not required but do remember to save it using an appropriate name.
- If the facility for changing text style is available on your system, experiment with different styles, sizes and line thicknesses.

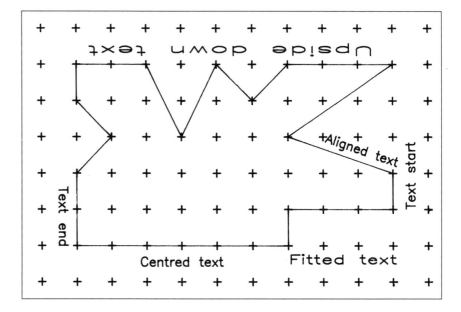

▶ **Figure 4.3** Adding text to a design

When you feel able to cope with text entry, read through the objectives and practical requirements of Task 4.4. The task combines text entry with the skills you have already learned. This is the first workbook design – perhaps your first CAD design – so it is worth giving it time and care.

Task 4.4 Creating standard drawing sheets

- Create an A4 size standard drawing sheet based on that given on the drawing on page 11. The essential features of the drawing sheet should, where possible, be as follows:

  a 10 mm border
  a title block size of no more than 160 mm × 40 mm
  white, continuous lines on 'black' background
  automatic orthogonal axes
  a point capture spacing of 10 mm
  a grid spacing of 10 mm × 10 mm
  exist on the default layer.
- Save the drawing sheet design for future use – the name for the design will be constrained by the particular CAD system in use, but it should contain a meaningful reference to an A4 sheet.
- Now create an A3 size prototype drawing sheet that has the same features as the A4 sheet you have just produced.
- Save this drawing sheet design for future use. Remember to use a name that refers to an A3 sheet.

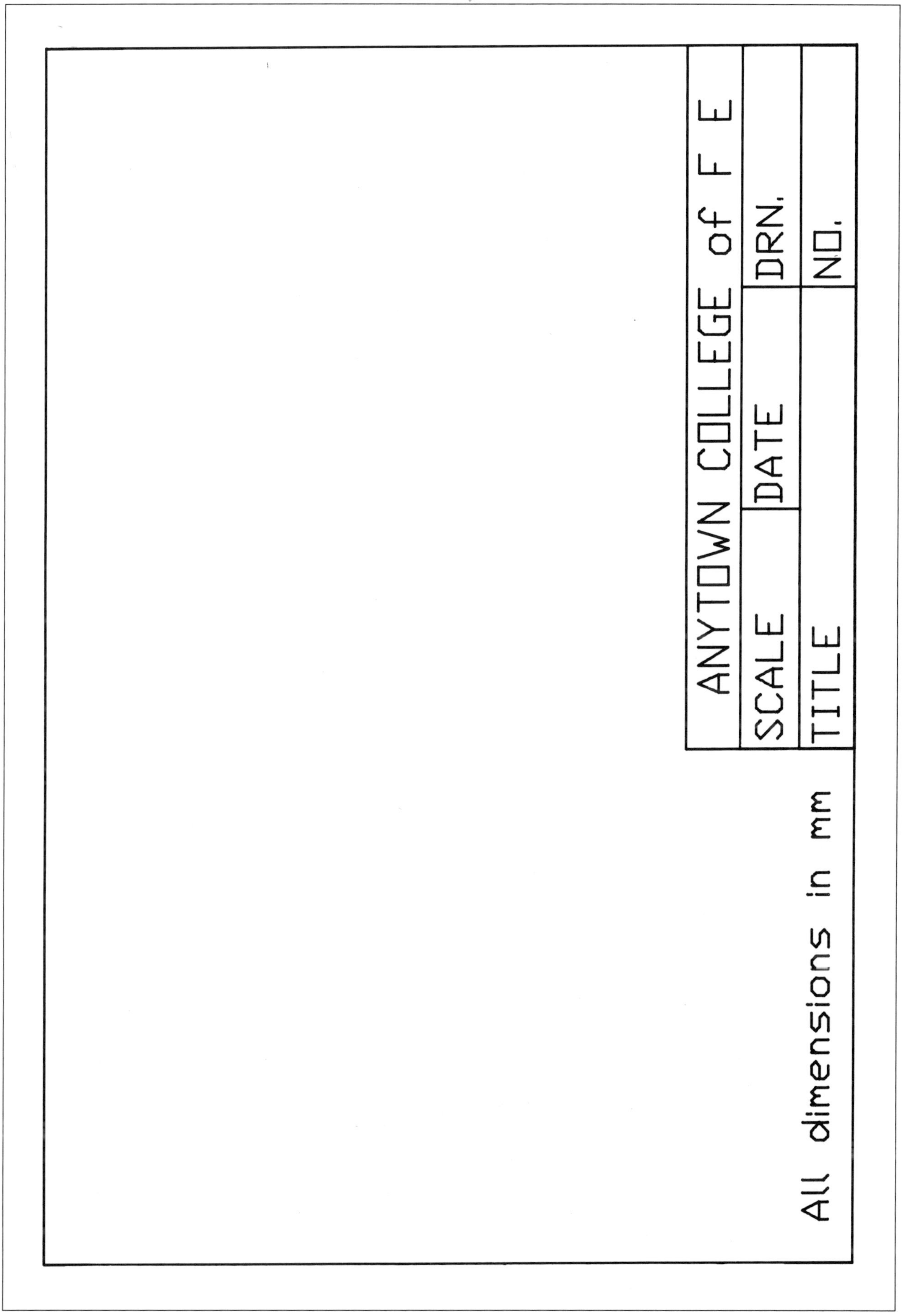

▲ **Figure 4.4** Drawing for Task 4.4

Using arcs, circles and lines

Many designs use curved lines, and CAD systems support this requirement in varying ways. If you are a new CAD user, you may become confused because a particular CAD system will draw all arcs in one angular direction, either clockwise or anti-clockwise. The arc will then be concave or convex depending on the starting point and until you become used to your system, you may find that you have to redraw arcs.

When drawing an arc by hand, you use the position of the centre and the length of the radius. As you will find with circles, however, CAD systems provide several methods. Figure 5.1 shows a selection of these.

▶ **Figure 5.1** Creating arcs

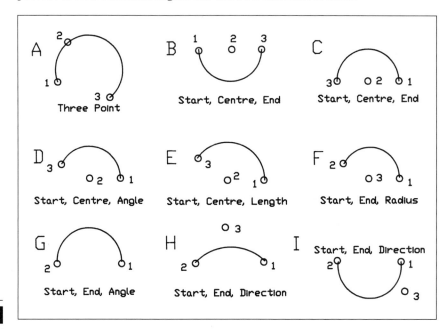

USEFUL OBSERVATION

Find out which of these arc commands, and any others, are on your system. Practise their use before reading further. Note that each command produces the same result but the different commands are used in different situations.

Circles are usually defined by specifying the centre and the radius or diameter. On a CAD system, there may be at least two additional methods. Examples are shown in Figure 5.2.

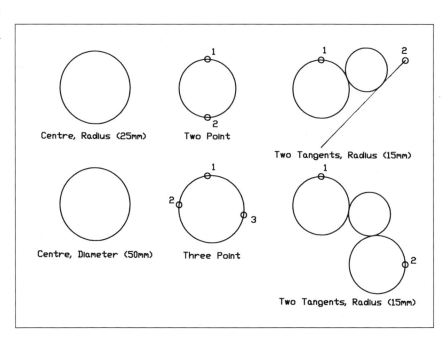

▶ **Figure 5.2** Creating circles

Task 5.1 Creating arcs and circles

Try to create arcs and circles by using all the methods illustrated in Figures 5.1 and 5.2. If there are other arc- and circle-creation methods on your system, use them as well.

Additional information

CONTINUE is a feature that is usually provided for both the ARC and the LINE commands. It allows a line or arc to be continued from the end of the previous line or arc. A mixture of these entities can then be drawn.

The following task requires you to use the arc and circle features of your system and combine them with the line drawing options that you have already used. The robot arm design to be copied for the task (Figure 5.3) was drawn using only these features.

Task 5.2 Using arcs, circles and lines

- Enter the CAD system and load the A4 standard drawing sheet created in Task 4.4.
- Dis-enable the point capture, orthogonal and grid options.
- Copy the robot arm design shown in Figure 5.3 by using arcs, circles, lines and, if available, the CONTINUE feature. (*Note:* There are several places where part of an arc or line ought to be erased, but you may leave this until the necessary technique has been introduced. Figure 9.2 shows what can be achieved at this later stage.)
- When you have finished the design, use the TEXT command to complete the details in the title block.
- Save the design, giving it an appropriate name.

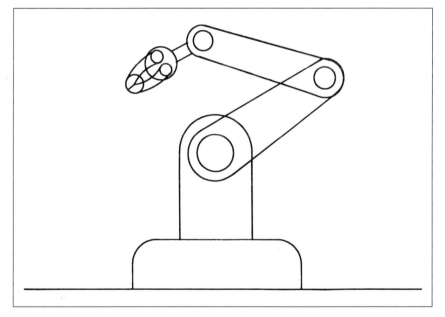

◀ **Figure 5.3** Using arcs, circles and lines

Learning Assignment 6

Using CAD drawing aids

Drawing aids have been referred to already, including point location and capture, ruled and orthogonal axes and a feature known as 'dragging'. If you specify a circle's centre and then move the pointing device, you can 'drag' the outside of the circle, centred on the specified point, to the required size. (The circle will be drawn as normal if you input the radius or diameter value.) If the pick button is pressed when the circle size looks correct, the dragged circle will be drawn at that size.

Moving the pointing device after defining a point for a line or multi-line will produce a similar feature called 'rubber-banding' – the movement of the pointing device will stretch a straight line from that point. When the position and length of the line look right, use the pick button to draw that line. Rubber-banding and point capture on the grid points allow drawings to be made quickly; these features were used to draw the design of Figure 4.1. A design may be drawn 'freehand' or, by using point co-ordinate or capture values, as accurately as desired.

TASKS

Task 6.1 Basic drawing aids

- Figure 6.1 was drawn using these aids. Create this design, which is based on a point capture and grid value of 5 mm, using an A4 size drawing sheet. Arcs, circles and lines should be dragged to the appropriate position before being picked.
- Save this drawing for future use. Remember to use and record a suitable name.

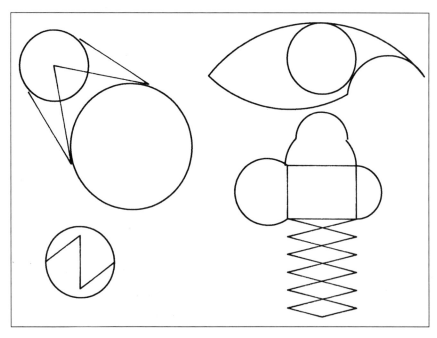

▶ **Figure 6.1** Drawing aid exercise

In Task 6.1, the point capture and grid values were equal at 5 mm, but on some CAD systems unequal values of *x* and *y* are allowed. Rotation of the grid about a defined point is also possible.

Figure 6.2 shows these features in use. Before rotation of the screen, the grid and point capture values are set at 20 mm horizontal and 30 mm vertical.

The screen rotation is 30° (anti-clockwise by convention) and orthogonal (right-angled) axes are selected. As a result, squares/rectangles and pointer crosshairs are all inclined at 30° to the horizontal and all lines will be drawn at either 30° or 120° (90° plus 30°).

14

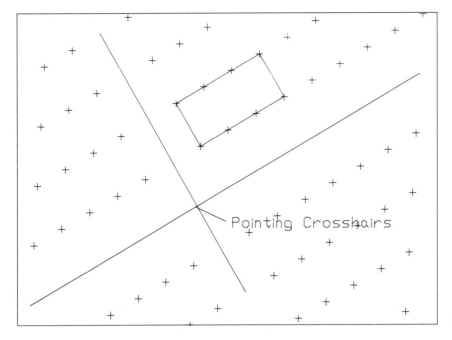

◀ **Figure 6.2** Additional drawing aids

Find out if any of these features are on your system. If so, practise using them by copying the two shapes shown in Figure 6.3. Here the rotation angle is 45° but the other drawing aids, excepting orthogonal axes, are the same as in Figure 6.2.

In Figure 6.3, the shape on the left was drawn without using orthogonal axes and so it was possible to draw lines 1, 2 and 3. The shape on the right was drawn when using orthogonal axes and so lines 1, 2 and 3 cannot be drawn. Because all lines have to be mutually at 90°, line 1 can only be replaced by one of the two dashed lines; the position is similar for lines 2 and 3.

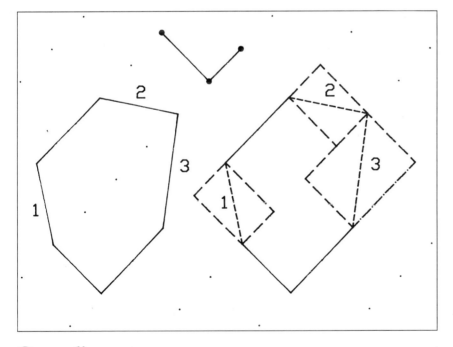

◀ **Figure 6.3** Using Rotate and Orthogonal features

Co-ordinate types

The default origin of the co-ordinate system used to define position is usually the bottom left-hand corner of the design screen. By graphical convention, the first of the two values to be stated is the horizontal or 'x' value – it is the left-to-right distance across the screen. The second value is the vertical or 'y' value, and gives the bottom-to-top distance.

Thus the origin is at position 0,0 and, for an A4-scaled design screen, the top right-hand corner will have the co-ordinate value of 297,210 mm.

Additional information

It is usual for the pointer's current co-ordinate value to be displayed in a status line; this line may also indicate whether features such as point capture, point location or orthogonal axes have been selected. When the pointing device is moved, the indicated value of the co-ordinates will change. If the measurement accuracy is suitable, the displayed co-ordinates can be used to select the desired points for the design.

You can usually place the origin of a co-ordinate system at any position you choose. If the origin is defined at the centre of the design screen, moving the pointer to the left or downwards from the screen centre gives negative co-ordinate values.

The redefining of co-ordinate system origins has more value in three-dimensional CAD, but that subject is outside the scope of this workbook. You must understand negative co-ordinates fully before you can use relative co-ordinates correctly.

A CAD system interprets a **relative co-ordinate** as being relative to the last specified point. It will recognise that a character such as '@' or 'R' in front of the x and y values will identify a relative co-ordinate. Negative x and/or y values mean that the line will be drawn to the left and/or downwards respectively from the last point.

Any x,y value without a non-numeric character in front, or elsewhere, will be identified by the CAD system as an **absolute co-ordinate**. The values of x and y are measured from the origin of the co-ordinate system in use. Negative values will usually produce an error message from the CAD system.

Two numbers separated by '<' are identified as **polar co-ordinates**, and there may also be a leading character. The first number is the line length and the second is the angle of that line from the zero angle direction, usually the 3 o'clock position. Angles are generally measured in degrees but other units may be used.

TASKS

ADDITIONAL TASKS

You may already know how your CAD system implements co-ordinate entry using the three methods introduced above. If not, create the design shown in Figure 6.4 using each of the three methods.

Figure 6.4 shows a design that can be created using any of the co-ordinate systems detailed above. As an exercise, attempt to create the design using each of the three systems. Remember that with relative and polar co-ordinates, the design can be created either clockwise or anti-clockwise.

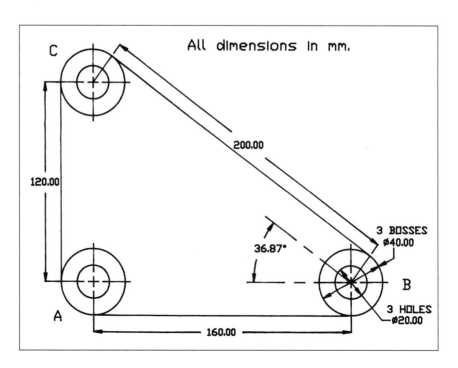

▶ **Figure 6.4** Use of point co-ordinates

You should not have any problems when creating these designs. If you do, however, you will find the information for positioning the three points, starting at co-ordinate 50,50 (point A) in each case, listed in the table below. Only anti-clockwise data is given, but you should not have difficulty in calculating the clockwise data.

CO-ORDINATE VALUES FOR FIGURE 6.4			
Co-ordinate system	Point A	Point B	Point C
Absolute	50.00,50.00 50.00,50.00	210.00,50.00	50.00,170.00
Relative	50.00,50.00 R0,−120.00	R160.00,0	R−160.00,120
Polar	50.00,50.00 R120.00<270.00	R160.00<0	R200.00<143.13

TASKS *ADDITIONAL TASK*

Load your standard A4 drawing sheet. Now, using one of the co-ordinate value sets given for Figure 6.4, create that design. Notice that a two-decimal place precision has been used for length and angular measurements.

Reference has been made to the use of rulers in the creation of designs. Variation in editing screen design may put a vertical ruler at either side of the screen and a horizontal ruler at the top or bottom. If a ruler feature is available on the CAD system, it should appear on both axes.

The ruler markings may match the point capture settings, or may be a multiple or sub-multiple of them. Extra-long markers can be used to indicate whole inches or centimetres, just like the rulers that are used in offices and workshops.

If the ruler markings match the grid points, you do not need to count the number of grid points when 'roughing out' a design. The ruler feature may be switched off without losing the previous setting.

TASKS ## Task 6.2 Using CAD system drawing aids

Before you begin any design task,

- think about what is to be drawn (for this task, look at Figure 6.5)
- decide what size of drawing sheet to use
- set up, to suit the design, the following:
  drawing units and precision – length and angle
  drawing limits for the sheet
  line width, type, colour
  point capture, grid, ruler values
  layers
  text size and style.

- Now you are ready to begin this task. Enter the CAD system and load a standard drawing sheet.
- Enable, and set correctly, those features of the CAD system that you consider necessary for the creation of the design shown in Figure 6.5. (Remember the possible minimum value of the upper limit co-ordinates.)
- Create the design shown in Figure 6.5. You may need to change the precision of the length and angle units.
- When you have finished the design, use the TEXT command to complete the details in the title block.
- Save the design under an appropriate name. Take care to preserve the standard drawing sheet for future use.

POINTS TO NOTE

If you are using a two-decimal place precision, remember that you must not correct an angular value to one decimal place. For example, all angles between 36.85° and 36.94° inclusive are taken to equal 36.9° when corrected to one decimal place. If an angle of 36.9° is input, the CAD system will interpret this as 36.90° and any later CAD system calculations involving angles might then contain errors.

It has been mentioned that CAD systems usually put 0° at the 3 o'clock position. Positive angular increase is by anti-clockwise rotation to give 90° at 12 o'clock, 270° (or −90°) at 6 o'clock, and so on.

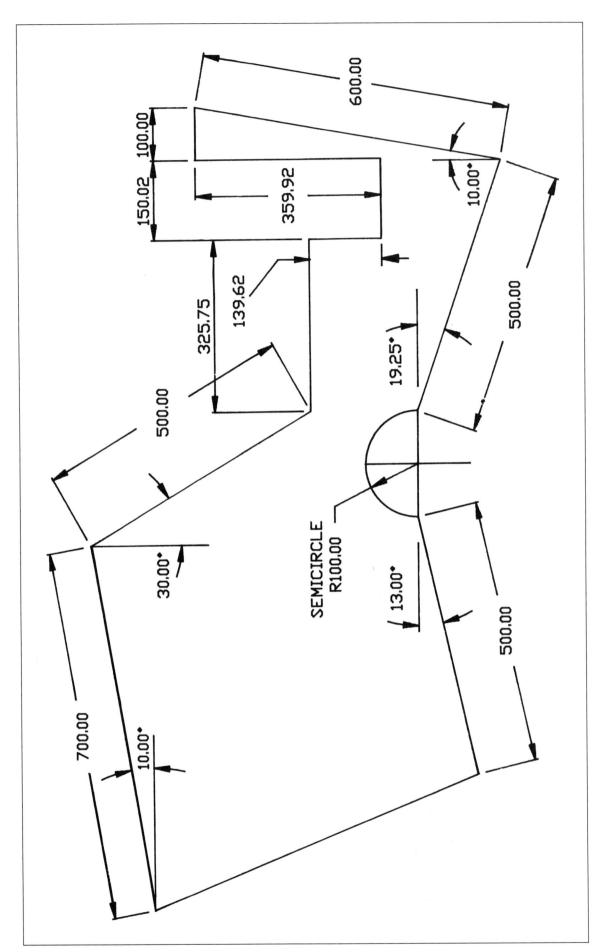

▲ **Figure 6.5** Drawing for Task 6.2

Learning Assignment 7

More CAD drawing aids

Zooming

When completing Task 6.2, you probably realised that it is difficult to work with distances of a few drawing units when the drawing limits are a thousand times larger. Most CAD systems overcome the problem by magnifying parts of the screen display – this is called the 'zooming' feature.

Different zoom facilities are offered by the various CAD systems. They include variable or fixed zoom factors, selection of a portion of the screen by using a 'window' and zooming the design to fill the screen. Now see an example of what ZOOM can do.

Figures 7.1a to 7.1e show a series of zooms on a design to indicate how very fine detail can exist even though the complete design cannot show that detail.

The blur inside the small rectangle of Figure 7.1a gets larger with successive zooms until, in Figure 7.1d, you can see that it consists of a square containing four lines of text.

Figure 7.1e shows that the single letter 'A' in the second line of the text contains even finer detail.

Task 7.1 Use of ZOOM features

In this task, you will re-create the design shown on Figure 7.1 and then add even finer detail. The dimensions are not required, and exact positioning of rectangles, squares and text is not necessary.

- Load your A4 drawing sheet, and then draw the 125×90 mm rectangle in the central area of the sheet. Now use your CAD system's ZOOM feature to expand the rectangle so that it fills the screen area.
- Draw the 50×25 rectangle in the central area of the screen and then expand it to fill the screen. Then draw, again in the central area, the 15×5 rectangle.
- Repeat this process of drawing and expanding until you have produced 'C&G 230' inside the letter 'A' (see Figure 7.1e. Now expand the '0' of '230' and draw four rectangles of decreasing size, inside it. Draw the second rectangle inside the first, the third inside the second and the fourth inside the third. Finally add the text 'TASK 7.1' inside the smallest rectangle.
- Now return to the original drawing sheet by reversing the ZOOM process, using the features available on your CAD system.

A POINT TO NOTE
To write the small size text, you may have to increase the number of decimal places that your CAD system works to. It is normal for text and curves to be shown as a series of short, straight lines as the zoom factor is increased.

The regeneration of a zoomed display can take a comparatively long time. This time depends upon the computer system's speed as well as being a function of the CAD software. The speed of regeneration can be increased, however, if the CAD system has 'dynamic zoom', which allows specified areas to be zoomed more quickly than normal.

Additional information

A 'pan' feature is available on some systems (the term comes from the cinema industry). With pan, the design can be moved around the screen. You can look for, or place, a particular item of interest. Pan also allows you to move a zoomed area in any direction and so display a different part of the zoomed design.

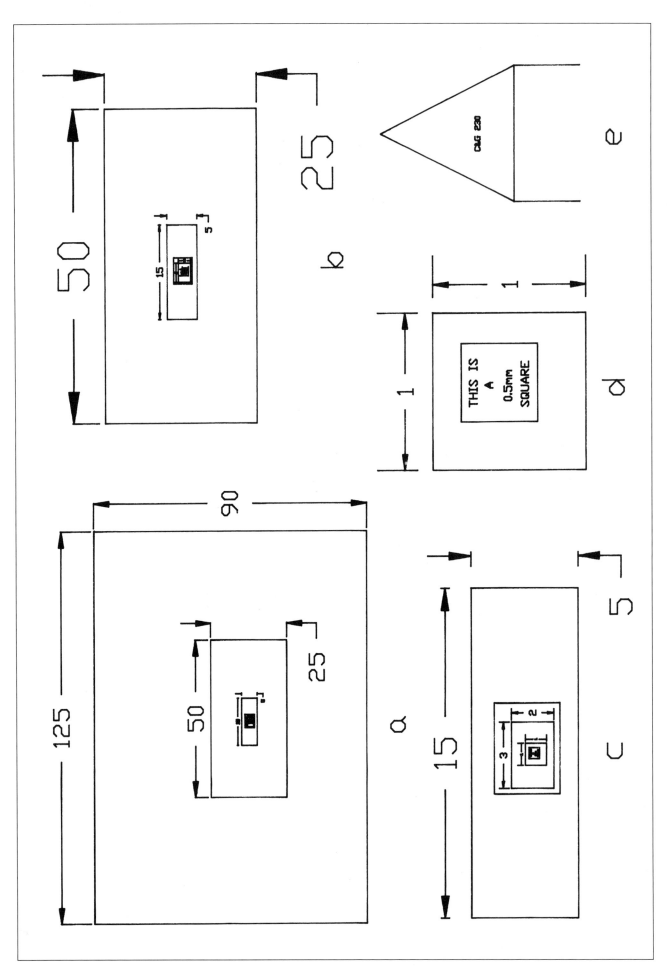

▲ **Figure 7.1** Illustrations of ZOOM

Layers

Using layers for drawing has been mentioned before. You can best appreciate their value if you think of them as transparent drawing sheets. When the sheets are stacked, all the creation details on the various layers are displayed. Without a colour monitor, however, layers cannot be fully exploited.

Obviously, construction lines are not required on the final drawing so, once those lines have been used, the construction layer can be frozen and it becomes invisible. If the text layer is frozen it will not have to be regenerated after zooming or redrawing. Freezing unwanted layers before regeneration therefore saves time, because systems will not normally accept 'change of mind' commands once regeneration commences.

The CAD standards within an organisation usually specify such details as special layer names, what the layers are used for, the linestyle to be used, the layer's colour and so on.

POINTS TO NOTE

Colour and layers may be of benefit only during the design activity, as plotted output will consist of black lines on white paper unless a colour plotter is available.

It is not easy to place a value on colours or layers. Some CAD systems do not provide them, and some designers do not use them even if they are available.

TASKS

Task 7.2 Use of layers and colours

You are asked to create the design shown in Figure 7.6, which is the outline of a floppy disc, of the size known as a '5¼ inch', although the design dimensions are given in millimetres. Such a simple design would not normally need construction lines or as many layers as we have indicated, but they are used here to demonstrate the value of layers in building up a series of composite designs. (Clearly, you can only carry out this task if you have layers and colours on your system!)

First load the standard A4 drawing sheet. Then set up layers with the parameters as shown in the table.

Layer name	Layer colour	Linetype
Outline	White	Continuous
Construction	Yellow	Hidden
Dimension 1	Green	Continuous
Dimension 2	Green	Continuous
Dimension 3	Green	Continuous
Text	Cyan	Continuous
Centre	Red	Centre
Holes	White	Continuous
Title	Cyan	Continuous

Layer names, like those given, should identify the use of the layer so that the design task is made easier. The colours may be left to personal preference but the linetypes are usually standardised for the type of drawing being produced.

In Figures 7.2 to 7.6 inclusive, each design was created by combining the indicated layers.

On a system supporting layers, you should be able to create all of the layer illustrations shown here. With a colour monitor, the advantages of layers plus colour should be self-evident.

POINTS TO NOTE

Task 7.3 gives you a chance to practise the use of layers, colours and linetypes. You should always follow the normal working practice of your own organisation concerning layer names, colours and linetypes, where this exists. If there is no policy, use the layer details given previously as a guide.

Figures 7.8a to 7.8d show possible layer contents.

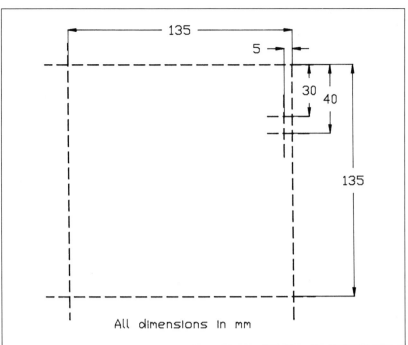

All dimensions in mm

▶ **Figure 7.2** Construction and Dimension 1 layers

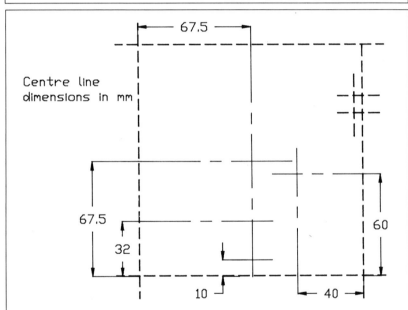

Centre line dimensions in mm

▶ **Figure 7.3** Construction, Centre and Dimension 2 layers

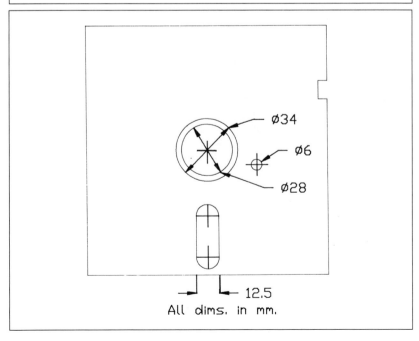

Ø34
Ø6
Ø28

12.5
All dims. in mm.

▶ **Figure 7.4** Outline, Holes and Dimension 3 layers

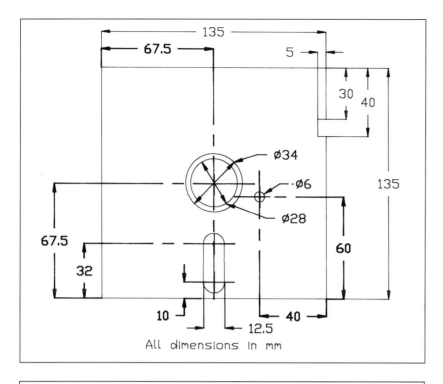

All dimensions in mm

◀ **Figure 7.5** Outline, Holes, Text and three Dimension layers

A 5¼" FLOPPY DISC

◀ **Figure 7.6** Outline, Holes and Title layers

Task 7.3 Using layers, colours and linetypes

- Enter the CAD system and load a standard drawing sheet.
- Enable, and set correctly, those features of the CAD system that you consider necessary for the creation of the design shown in Figure 7.7.
- Create the design shown in Figure 7.7. Remember that the contents of a layer might be used only during the creation of the design, and need not necessarily appear on the final design.
- Using the text layer, complete the text details for the design.
- When you have finished the design, use the TEXT command to complete the details in the title block.
- Save the design, using an appropriate name – take care to preserve the standard drawing sheet for future use.

▼ **Figure 7.7** Drawing for Task 7.3

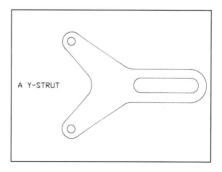

A Y-STRUT

23

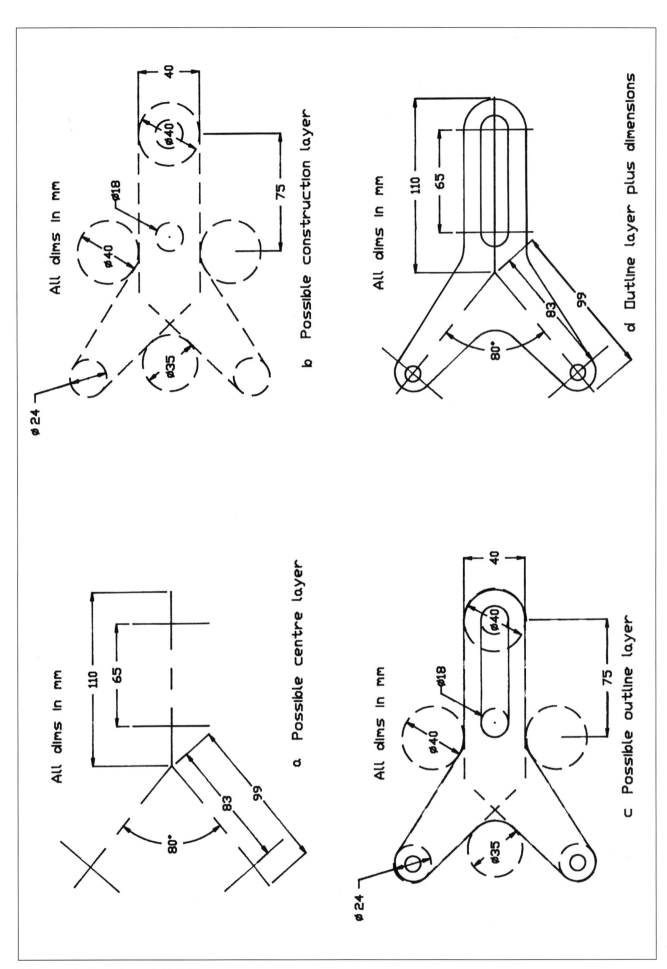

▲ **Figure 7.8** Layers for use in Task 7.3

Learning Assignment 8

Fillets and chamfers

Filleting

In Figure 7.8c, you may have wondered why the arcs at the intersection of two straight lines (normally called fillets) were constructed using circles. The reason is that easy fillet creation on a CAD system had still to be dealt with at that stage. This did not prevent the fillets from being drawn, but CAD systems can deal with fillet creation more efficiently than this.

When you are creating fillets by hand, you draw a circle or arc to just blend with the two lines being filleted. This is the 'longhand' method that was used in Figure 7.8c. This is not an efficient method to use on a CAD system and it would be easier if the two lines to be filleted were identified either before or after keying in the value of the fillet radius. This is the method which is in common use on CAD systems, and which is probably used on your system.

TASKS

Task 8.1 Filleting

Figure 8.1a shows a multi-line drawing with acute, obtuse and right angles to which fillets of differing radii are to be fitted.

When filleting, the CAD system will ask for the fillet radius, and also for an identification of the two lines to be filleted. The order of these requests will depend on the CAD system used, and in this workbook we cannot be too specific.

Create the profile shown in Figure 8.1a for the following fillet command exercise.

Figure 8.1b shows all the two-line junctions that require filleting using a 5 mm radius.

Some CAD systems automatically check the validity of a fillet request; invalid requests will be rejected. Figure 8.1c shows what happens if the fillet radius is 10 mm. Carry out this procedure and test the result for yourself.

In the right-hand part of the design, the right angle should be rejected but the obtuse angle will fillet correctly. Note that this does not depend, as might be thought, on the order of filleting. Other CAD systems, yours included, may treat this request differently.

As you might expect, a radius of more than 10 mm will be rejected for that right angle and the adjacent obtuse angle. Figure 8.1d shows the results of such an attempt.

Chamfering

An obvious follow-on to filleting is the chamfering of line pairs; CAD systems usually offer varying degrees of sophistication to this feature.

It is desirable to be able to chamfer at angles other than 45°, and this is achieved by requesting an input of picked points or a pair of numeric values.

TASKS

Task 8.2 Chamfering

Apply the chamfer command to the design of Figure 8.1a as shown in Figure 8.2. (Note that unequal dimension chamfers are used.)

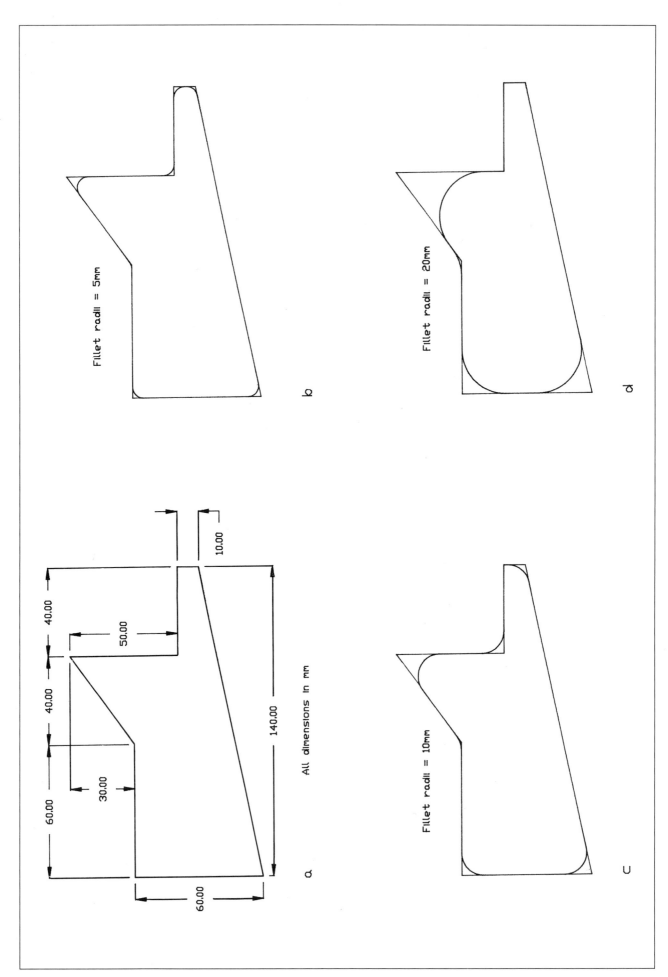

▲ Figure 8.1

26

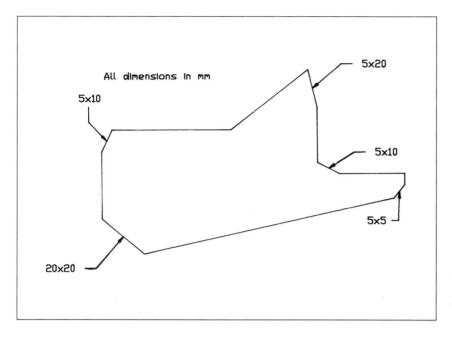

All dimensions in mm

5x20

5x10

5x10

5x5

20x20

◀ **Figure 8.2** Various chamfer values for Task 8.2

Task 8.3 Using fillets and chamfers

- Enter the CAD system and load a standard drawing sheet.
- Enable, and set correctly, those features of the CAD system that you consider necessary for the creation of the design shown in Figure 8.3.
- Create the design shown in Figure 8.3. Remember that the contents of the construction layer should be used only for the creation of the design, and should not appear on the final design.
- Using the text layer, complete the text details for the design and the title block.
- Save the design, using an appropriate name – take care to preserve the standard drawing sheet for future use.

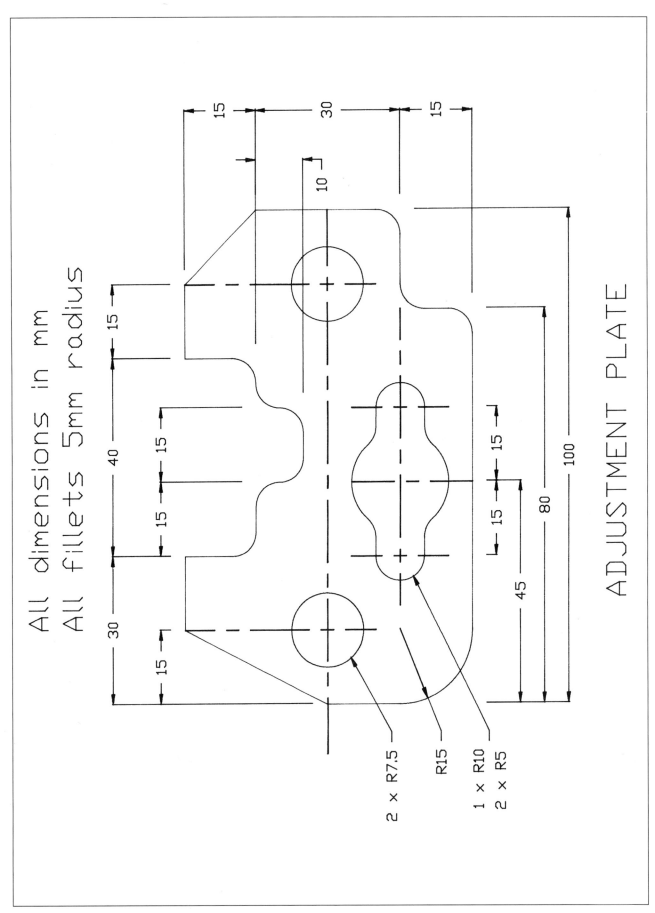

All dimensions in mm
All fillets 5mm radius

ADJUSTMENT PLATE

2 × R7.5

R15

1 × R10

2 × R5

▲ **Figure 8.3**   Drawing for Task 8.3

Learning Assignment 9

Array and other editing features

Object capture

In Task 8.3, you may have met problems in removing the unwanted parts of the three circles that make up the composite hole in the plate. From the commands that have been dealt with so far, you probably used LINE, ZOOM, ERASE and, perhaps, OBJECT CAPTURE or SNAP to produce the final design.

Object capture is a feature that has been referred to previously in this workbook without a detailed explanation. If you did use the feature, you obviously know how your CAD system implements it. If not, the following information is important.

Point capture, as you have seen, concerns the locking of the crosshairs on to a grid point setting. Object capture refers to the capture of an entity or part of a drawing. This may take place at the end or the middle of a picked line, at the centre of a circle or arc, at the drawing point nearest to the crosshairs, at the intersection of two lines or arcs, and so on. Some systems allow you to combine types to allow the capture of different point types without changing the selection in between.

Typical object capture types are listed below; compare them with those available on your CAD system:

nearest (visually closest point)
endpoint (of closest line or arc)
midpoint (of line or arc)
centre (of arc or circle)
quadrant (of arc or circle – 0, 90, 180 or 270°)
intersection (of two lines, line and arc or circle, two circles and/or arcs)
perpendicular (normal between object and the last point)
tangent (tangent to object and the last point).

This list may differ from the one on your CAD system. Time and use will show you whether the differences are important.

> *A POINT TO NOTE*
> As with point capture, altering the CAD system variables will fix how close the crosshairs have to be to the desired point. Using this feature with zoom allows the more effective capturing of object features.

Task 9.1 Object capture

TASKS

Figure 9.1 can be used to find the object capture types that your CAD system supports. Note that type names may be different.

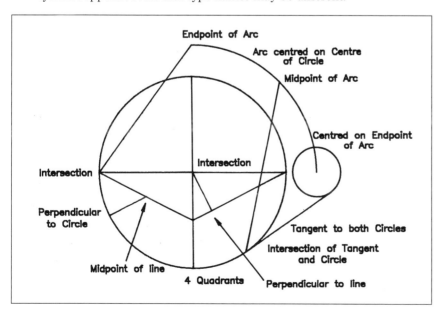

◀ **Figure 9.1** Object capture exercise

29

TASKS
Using object capture, draw the geometric figure on your A4 drawing sheet. Although the dimensions are not important, you should note the types of object capture that produce similar results to those shown. Then complete the title block and save the design using a meaningful name.

Partial erase

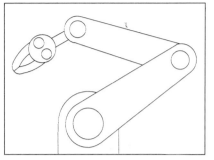

▲ **Figure 9.2** Use of partial erase command

When Task 5.2 was set, this workbook had introduced only a few CAD commands. Because of this, your final drawing of the robot arm (Figure 5.3) included some lines that should have been hidden from view. For example, the arc at the top of the vertical column was one entity and so could not be partially erased at the place where the large arm obscured it. CAD systems may solve this problem by using a command that breaks the entity into two parts.

The effect of using this type of command on the robot arm design of Task 5.2 is shown in Figure 9.2.

TASKS
Task 9.2 Partial erase

- Retrieve your drawing for Task 5.2.
- Set object capture to 'nearest', then call up 'partial erase' before locking on to the arc to be deleted between the two sides of the arm on your drawing. (This will probably identify the arc in some way.) Set object capture to 'intersection', and then pick one of the two places where the arc intersects with the arm. The arc between those two points should be erased.
- Repeat the operation with the other part of the arc that is between the arm sides.
- Now use partial erase on the remaining unwanted lines. When you have finished, save the complete drawing as a second version of the robot arm design.

Hatching

Some CAD systems give only a few hatch patterns, others give a wide choice. On the more advanced systems you can create your own patterns.

Figure 9.3 shows three areas that were hatched with the same pattern but using different hatch scale values.

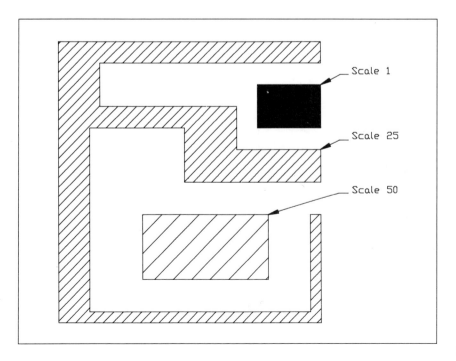

▶ **Figure 9.3** Hatching of areas

Hatching on a CAD system can only work correctly if all the boundary line parts intersect; problems may arise if the boundary line overhangs or has a break. Some CAD systems allow internal areas to remain unhatched. Figure 9.4 shows one possible result of this feature.

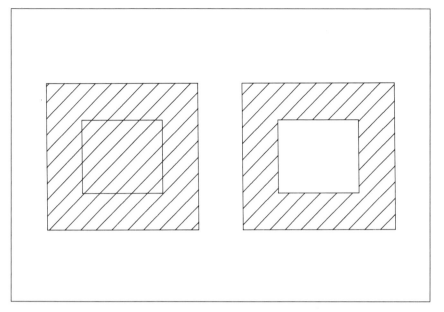

◀ **Figure 9.4** Hatching variations

Copying and moving

The introductory section of this workbook claimed that CAD saves time. The hatch feature is a good example of this. The next two features, the 'copying' and the 'moving' of a set of entities to another part of the design screen, will also promote drawing efficiency.

These two features usually apply to text as well as line drawings. The repositioning or duplication of text within a drawing is a common requirement.

The COPY command allows you to repeat a set of selected entities wherever required in the drawing. (When you are copying to create an array or circular design, it is better to use a different command; this will be dealt with later.)

Task 9.3 Copying

- On an A4 drawing sheet, create the entity set in the position shown in Figure 9.5.
- Using the COPY command, change this entity set into the geometrical pattern shown in Figure 9.6. The set of entities should now be identified, either by individual picking or using an enclosing 'window'. (A window feature is very useful and is found on most CAD systems.)
- Pick a datum point for the pattern to be copied ; this may be called a 'handle'. Then enter the location point for the new copy position to give a duplicate entity set as shown in Figure 9.7.

▲ **Figure 9.5** Set of entities to be copied

Additional information

You may have used a total of nine COPY commands on the entity in Figure 9.5 to give the result shown in Figure 9.6. This number could be reduced by selecting a larger number of entities at an intermediate point.

In Figure 9.7 the COPY command has been used with a window, shown as a dotted box, for entity selection. When COPY is called, the 'new' entities may be rubber-banded – see the dotted lines between the corners of the two windows.

▲ **Figure 9.6** Using COPY to create a new design

31

A POINT TO NOTE

The design in Figure 9.6 does *not* form an 'array' as defined in CAD systems.

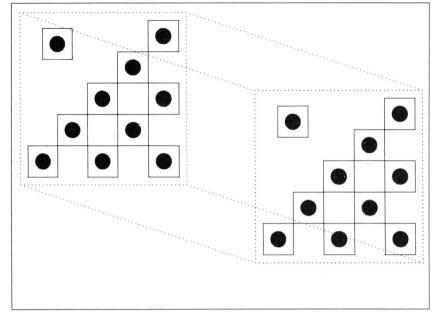

▶ **Figure 9.7** Using COPY to create a repeated design

Having used COPY to make a new design, its final position may need to be changed slightly. This could be achieved by erasing that design and using COPY again.

Task 9.4 Moving

TASKS

Another way is to use the MOVE command. You identify the entity set that is to be moved, indicate the datum point and then indicate the new drawing position for that datum.

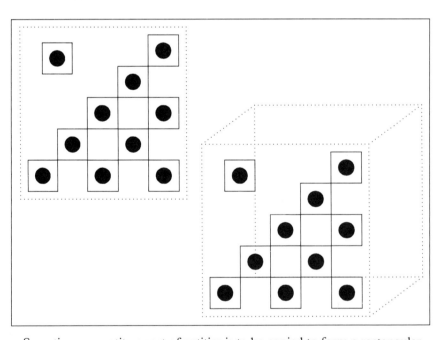

▶ **Figure 9.8** Using MOVE on a set of entities

USEFUL OBSERVATION

Figure 9.8 shows, using dotted lines, the movement that took place. Again, a window identifies the relevant entities.

Sometimes an entity or set of entities is to be copied to form a rectangular or circular pattern. Some CAD systems provide an ARRAY command to create such regular layouts very quickly. For example, suppose that a solid metal block is to be made lighter by drilling holes in one face. The designer would draw only one hole, and then use the ARRAY command to create a regular pattern of such holes.

A spoked wheel could be created from the design of only one spoke plus its hub and rim details – that design would then be copied by rotating through 360°. Figure 9.9a shows the construction and centre line details for one spoke of a twelve-spoke wheel. The spoke sides are produced by offsetting the spoke centre line by an appropriate amount – the angle of the arc, because there are twelve spokes, is 30°.

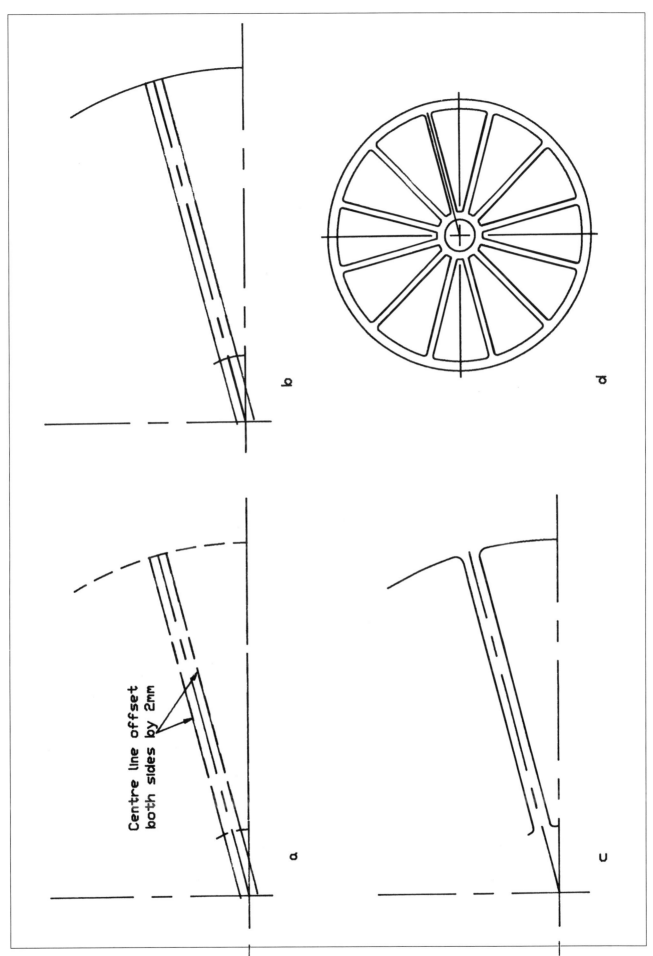

Centre line offset
both sides by 2mm

b

d

a

c

▲ **Figure 9.9** A twelve-spoke wheel design

On most CAD systems, the offset command for a line can be extended to complex polygons, and can include arcs, chamfers and so forth. Find out if the facility exists on your system and use it for this and other designs.

Figure 9.9b shows that the construction lines for the spoke are two arcs and two parallel lines (layers should be used).

To complete the basic spoke, the fillets are added *after* splitting the two arcs into four by removing the portions between the spoke sides. Figure 9.9c shows the final spoke design.

You can see, from Figure 9.9c, that a repetition of that design by eleven consecutive rotations of 30° will give the required twelve spokes. This rotation, plus the rim and the axle/hole, are shown in Figure 9.9d.

The command name used will be 'array' or something similar. This design used a 'polar' or 'circular' array; an array may also be 'rectangular'. The command structure depends, in both cases, on the CAD system in use.

TASKS *ADDITIONAL TASK*

Now create a wheel design based on Figure 9.9d but with a different number of spokes. Note that the number of spokes must divide *exactly* into 360°, to avoid precision problems. Use your A4 sheet and appropriate values for diameter, spoke thickness and fillet radii.

The next activity deals with the rectangular array feature. Figure 9.10 shows an array of seven rows of ten circles. This was produced by drawing the circle in the bottom left corner of the design and then calling the array-creation command.

You will have to identify the entity and then input details of the number of rows and their separation, plus the number of columns and their separation.

TASKS *ADDITIONAL TASK*

Create the design of Figure 9.10 as a means of gaining experience with the ARRAY command and of preparing for Task 9.5.

Task 9.5, the design of a components delivery carousel, should be attempted only when you are confident about using both the circular and rectangular array features.

TASKS ## Task 9.5 Using ARRAY and other editing features

- Enter the CAD system and load a standard drawing sheet.
- Enable, and set correctly, those features of the CAD system that you consider necessary for the creation of the design shown in Figure 9.11. Set the drawing limits after considering those dimensions that are given on the design. All the other dimensions are left to your discretion. (The design process is a very personal one. If you need guidance, however, you will find a suitable order of creation given after this task.)
- Create the design shown in Figure 9.11. Remember that the contents of, say, the construction layer should be used only for the creation of the design and should not appear on the final design. Before you place the components boxes on the spokes, save the design with a name that implies an intermediate design stage; this will be used later. Then complete the design.
- Using the text layer, complete all the text details that you consider necessary for the design.
- Save the design, using an appropriate name. It will be used later.

A POINT TO NOTE
You do not need to draw the outside of the wheel rim or the hub's axle/hole at this stage.

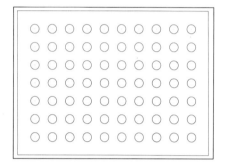

▲ **Figure 9.10** A rectangular array

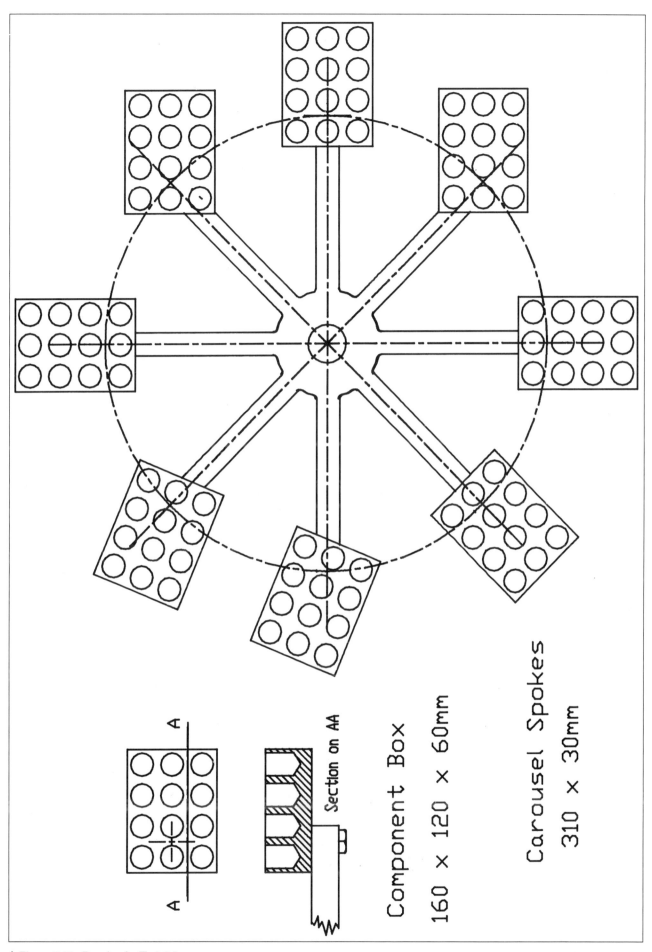

Component Box
160 × 120 × 60mm

Carousel Spokes
310 × 30mm

Section on AA

▲ **Figure 9.11** Drawing for Task 9.5

- Decide on the dimensions and limits you are going to use. Then use your Centre layer to lay out the centre lines for the spokes of the carousel. Leave enough space for the components box design.
- Use ZOOM to give the screen display shown in Figure 9.12. Use offset, arc and fillet to create the detail of the two adjacent half-spokes.

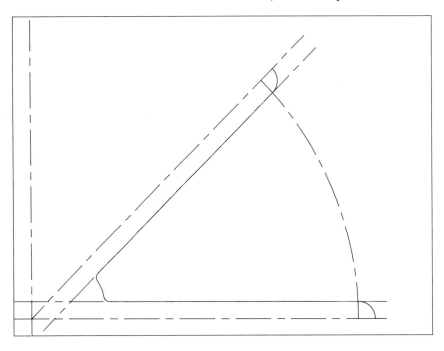

▶ **Figure 9.12** Spoke construction detail

- Use the correct ARRAY command(s) to create an eight-spoke wheel. Remember the centres for the components boxes.
- Complete the wheel details.
- Select the area for the components box design and draw the construction and centre lines on the appropriate layers.
- Use the correct ARRAY command(s) to create the component sockets.
- Create the sectioned view and hatch it correctly.
- Use the COPY command with the completed wheel and components box.
- Use the COPY command to position a components box on one of the spokes.
- Use the correct ARRAY command(s) to create a components box on each spoke. (Consider using the ARRAY option that aligns each box along a radial line.)
- If you know how the ROTATE feature works on your system, use it to re-align the appropriate boxes to take up the positions shown in Figure 9.11.
- Use the ZOOM and PARTIAL ERASE features of your system to remove those spoke details that are under the components boxes.
- Add the required text details and save the appropriate view.

Learning Assignment 10

Blocks

Another feature on some CAD systems is that you can save a set of entities for use on other designs at a later time. This means that a design, once created, should never have to be created again.

The usual name for the saved entity set is 'block', and libraries of standard blocks are in use in many CAD areas. A block can be rotated, positioned and expanded or reduced at will but you cannot normally edit the contents of a block – it is saved as a single entity. Using this feature, the components box in Task 9.5 could have been saved as a block and then re-inserted at the required angle for each spoke.

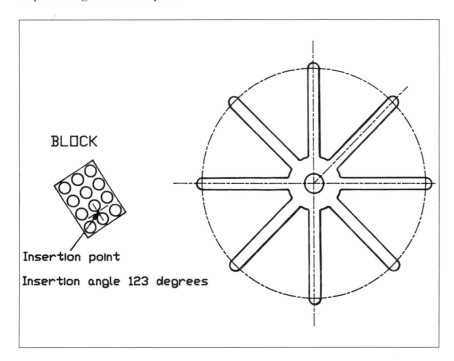

BLOCK

Insertion point

Insertion angle 123 degrees

◄ **Figure 10.1** Insertion of components box block

TASKS

ADDITIONAL TASK

As an exercise in using blocks, load in the intermediate design that was saved during Task 9.5. It should consist of the designs for the components box and the wheel.

Figure 10.1 was created by inserting a block containing the components box design into a drawing sheet containing the wheel design.

The usual procedure is to call block-creation, identify the insertion point and indicate the entities that are to be saved in the block.

The insertion point here is the centre of the attachment point of the box to a spoke; it is also the rotation axis for the box. A window can be used to select the twelve holes and the rectangle that form the components box design.

Having created the block, the CAD system may delete it from the display screen. The components box, which now exists as a block, can be placed in the wheel design, or any other design, by calling the insert-block feature.

In Figure 10.1, the block has been inserted at an arbitrary position and angle. It could, however, have been placed on one of the spokes at the correct angle.

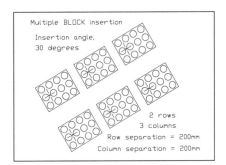

▲ **Figure 10.2** Multiple block insertion

Task 10.1 Block insertion

A block-insertion feature may include a rectangular array option that allows multiple insertions in one operation. This is shown in Figure 10.2.

If there is a multiple block-insertion feature on your CAD system, complete this exercise by creating the design shown in Figure 10.2.

The stretch feature

Figure 10.3 shows another time-saving feature of CAD systems, which allows size and shape to be changed without erasing and redrawing. One name of the feature is 'stretch', but it also allows items to be shortened. Non-orthogonal changes are possible on some CAD systems.

In Figure 10.3, view 1 shows a suggested layout of a garden and view 4 shows an alternative proposal. Views 2 and 3 show steps in changing view 1 to view 4 using the stretch feature.

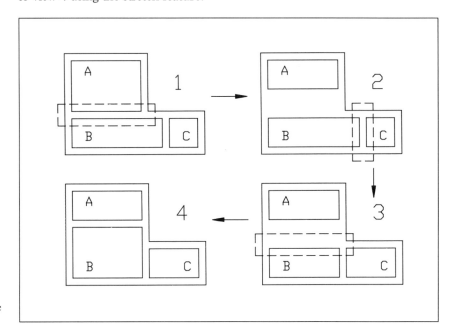

▶ **Figure 10.3** The shape stretching feature at work

A POINT TO NOTE

Not all CAD systems offer the same stretch facilities. Some may exclude the stretching of circles but allow the stretching of ellipses, arcs and complex shapes like those in Figure 10.4. The arrows show the direction and the amount of stretching.

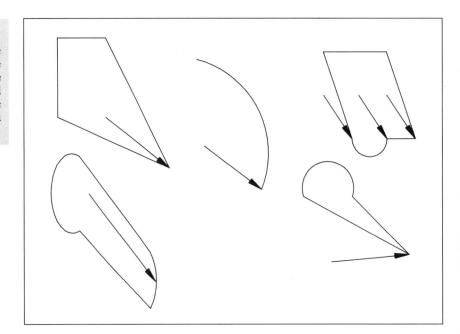

▶ **Figure 10.4** More shape stretching

Task 10.2 Stretching

As an exercise in using this command, consider part of a house plan that shows a wall with a door near one end of it. To reposition the door at the opposite end of the wall, the stretch feature can be used. If your CAD system supports the feature, create the wall/door design and then use the feature to change the door's position to the other end of the wall.

As a further exercise, create view 1 of Figure 10.3 and then use stretch to change it to look like view 4.

Dimensioning

Most CAD systems provide a variety of dimensioning options and allow you to alter the associated variables.

For example, the arrowhead may have a default size of 3 mm – quite acceptable on an A4 drawing, but less visible as the drawing sheet limits are extended. Or a dot or tick/check can replace the arrowhead, to suit users from other CAD disciplines. Also, the default text size will be too small on large-scale designs and too large on designs having fine detail. Figure 7.1 shows different text sizes on the same design.

Linear dimensioning can be horizontal, vertical, rotated or aligned with the measured entity. The horizontal, vertical and aligned dimension features in CAD are the same as those in traditional draughting.

Additional information

Some CAD systems will also allow you to change other factors, such as text position. For example, the text is usually centred in the dimension line, but on some systems it can be placed above the line. The CAD system may allow considerable dimensioning customisation – one system allows nearly forty changes.

Tolerancing is offered by some CAD systems and the user can supply unequal upper and lower values. Some systems provide an upper and lower limit value as the dimension.

This workbook cannot deal with all the many dimensioning variations between CAD systems, and you will need to find out what your own system provides. Company standards may prohibit any change even if customisation is possible.

Task 10.3 Dimensioning

You can now try your dimensioning skills on the workbook designs that you have created. Figure 6.4, for instance, has several dimension types. Load your saved version and dimension the relevant details. Try changing text/arrowhead sizes and the tolerance feature if your system supports it.

Task 10.4 Using dimensioning features

- Enter the CAD system and load the design that you saved on completion of Task 7.3, the Y-strut.
- Using your CAD system reference manual, set up those dimensioning features of the CAD system that you consider are necessary to dimension the Y-strut design fully.
- Save the dimensioned design, giving it an appropriate name – it will be used later.

User facilities

This Assignment deals with some non-drawing features that are available in a typical CAD system.

For example, if you are trying to find the cost of raw materials for a new design, you may need to find the area of a complex flat shape. Figure 11.1 shows such a shape.

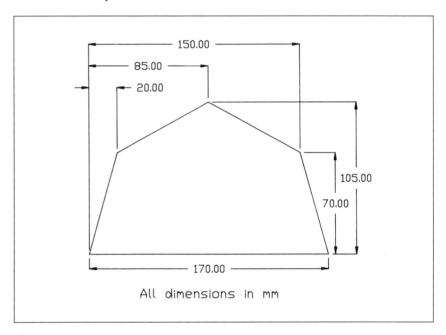

▶ **Figure 11.1** Basic shape for area calculation

The shape can be divided into four right-angled triangles and one rectangle. You can then use basic area calculations to find the total area (see Figure 11.2). The value, correct to two decimal places, is 12 775.00 mm^2.

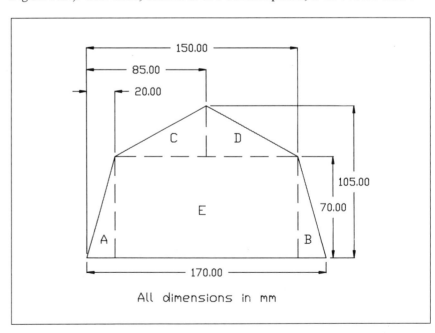

▶ **Figure 11.2** Shapes for manual area calculation

By using a CAD 'area' command, this answer could be obtained just by picking the shape's boundary. The boundary length, or perimeter, may be given also – 463.24 mm in this example. You can use aligned linear dimensioning to check this (see Figure 11.3).

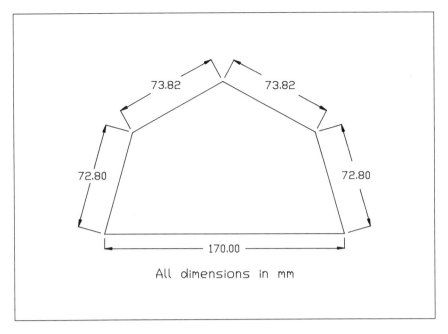

If the shape contains holes, the area of the holes is subtracted from the total surface area.

Such CAD features give this type of data without you having to complete a dimensioning exercise, since it comes from the same data that the CAD system uses for dimensioning.

Some systems will give you a long list of the drawing entities in the current design, plus details of the layers in use such as their colours, dimensions and text size. The system may also give the starting date of the current design and the actual time spent on it.

Task 11.1 User facilities

TASKS

As an exercise, find out if your system gives data on area, length and so on of the parts within a design. One way of doing this is to copy Figure 11.1 and then try to verify the values given earlier. Remember to use the same precision settings.

Additional information

With a CAD system, the building-up of a library of standard parts is a natural consequence of the design process, since the fast retrieval of standard items is made easy. A clever system for storing and retrieving the data is provided by a special computer program called a database management system, or DBMS.

Co-ordination and co-operation will be required to set up and use the DBMS efficiently. Basically, this means creating and using standard name types for parts, parts number types, symbols and so on. The modification and/or archiving of designs and the adding or deleting of items from a library of standard parts or symbols, will be restricted to certain staff; the use of passwords is the normal way of doing this.

TASKS

ADDITIONAL TASK

Now find out which features are on your system. This may be hard if the CAD system supports features unused by the company. Several reasons may exist for this, including ignorance of their existence or of their possible benefits. You may have to rely on the system reference manual for guidance.

Command menus for related CAD functions and help files for commands are usually provided by the CAD system; use these to find the answers to this exercise. A command name such as LIST might produce a parts listing - the LIST help file should say what the command does. One CAD system will index all its commands when you input '?', and the index can then be searched for likely command names.

A POINT TO NOTE

A particular menu may not be as useful to one user as it is to another, because the group of commands for a certain design activity may be very specific. As a designer, you will want command groups that make your CAD system most efficient for you. The more times a menu item is reselected, the slower the design process will be – this is more obvious to the experienced CAD user.

Some systems allow users to make up their own menus so that often-used commands can be grouped into one menu or placed into sub-menus. This is called 'customising' and includes the creation of 'standard' drawings.

Some CAD systems accept that international requirements differ; for example, different measuring systems and alternative spellings (such as 'centre' and 'center') are used in different countries. On some systems, you can select a UK-based menu instead of a US-based one, and the differences may be more than just spelling.

Another benefit to users of customisable systems is being able to create new commands. Such commands allow users to regularly create similar, but non-identical, design entities for which a block cannot be used; these may be called 'macro' or 'parametric' designs.

Some CAD systems use the word 'macro' to describe a parametric design feature. Other systems reserve the name for a set of CAD commands that carry out functions such as finding the mass of a body from its area, constant thickness and density.

TASKS | *ADDITIONAL TASK*

Find out if your CAD system supports a parametric design or macro feature such as the automatic creation of a 'bubble' with a user specifying position and text. Another example might be the duplication of a set of entities from one layer on to another. You may have to use the system reference manual to find what is available.

Exchanging drawing files

Organisations may need to use drawing files on other CAD systems at the same location, or even in other organisations, perhaps so that specialised work can be carried out on the design in various offices. To avoid the likely introduction of errors, the increase of costs and considerable duplication of effort, this must be done without having to re-create the drawing files manually.

To achieve this, all the data in a drawing file must be held in a structured form and organised in a standard format so that transfers between CAD systems can take place without compatibility problems occurring.

CAD systems provide a means of exchanging drawing files electronically using either the Initial Graphics Exchange Standard, or Specification, file format (known as IGES) or the Drawing Interchange (DXF) file format. Most CAD systems give users a choice between the two.

Additional information

The DXF format uses the standard ASCII text file format and is easily translated to other formats used by industry. The IGES format was produced to provide CAD/CAM compatibility via a standard interface. The sending CAD/CAM system uses a translator program called a 'pre-processor', and the receiving system then uses another translator program called a 'post-processor'.

It is usual to transfer the DXF data from the hard disc to a floppy disc, or magnetic tape, for manual transmission between organisations but it can be transmitted using a telephone system data link.

In the following task, you will simulate the transfer of drawing data. The procedure is the same for CAD systems that are in different countries as for those in the same building.

USEFUL OBSERVATION

Comparing the size of a drawing file and its DXF file shows that the DXF file will be about twice as long – this is for an accuracy of six decimal places for all positional co-ordinates. As an example, Figure 10.1 has a drawing file length of about 9 KBytes but the DXF version length is nearly 19 KBytes. When the DXF accuracy is increased from six decimal places to sixteen, the DXF version length increases to over 24 KBytes.

TASKS | ## Task 11.2 DXF files

- Enter the CAD system, and load the design that you saved on completion of Task 10.4.
- Add, in an appropriate position on the design, the text 'Task 11'.
- Use the command 'DXFOUT', or similar, to create a DXF format version of the design. Use the name 'TASK11'.

- Copy the file TASK11.DXF to a floppy disc. (You may need to ask for help to do this as some CAD systems may not support copying files to floppy disc.)
- If a second CAD system is available to you, use it to simulate one situated at a different location; if not, use your own CAD system. Copy the file TASK11.DXF from the floppy disc into the drawing area of the CAD system.
- Enter the CAD system and start a new drawing with the name TASK11.
- Use the DXFIN command to load the file TASK11.DXF. The drawing with the text 'Task 11' will be created on the screen.

ADDITIONAL TASKS

Create a new drawing that contains only a single straight line, a circle that is centred on one end of that line and a single word of text, such as 'lollipop'. Now create a DXF version of the screen design on a floppy disc and exit from the CAD system.

You may need help in the next part of this task which is to obtain a printout of the contents of the DXF file. The wordprocessing system should be loaded with the DXF file via the non-document, or programming, mode.

When you look at the printout, you will see that the file consists of four sections with the names 'Header', 'Tables', 'Blocks' and 'Entities' and ends with an End of File (EOF) line. The file is a textual description of a complete drawing file, including all the text on that file, and data on layers, colours, dimension precision, linetypes, etc.

An example of an 'empty' (no design data) DXF file printout is given below and this will allow you to identify where the various types of information regarding a CAD design are held.

You do not have to remember the details about the way in which the DXF file is organised, because you can consult the CAD system reference manual if necessary.

Structure of a DXF file

```
        0                          (Begin HEADER Section)
SECTION
        2
HEADER
        (Header variable items go here)
        0
ENDSEC                             (End HEADER Section)
        0                          (Begin TABLES Section)
SECTION
        2
TABLES
        0
TABLE
        2
LINETYPE
        70    (a group number – data on maximum table items)
        (linetype table items go here)
        0
ENDTAB
        0
TABLE
        2
LAYER (or STYLE, VIEW, etc.)
        70    (a group number)
        (layer, etc. table items go here)
        0
ENDTAB
        0
```

```
ENDSEC                                    (End TABLES Section)
   0                                      (Begin BLOCKS Section)
SECTION
   2
BLOCKS
         (block definition entries go here)
   0
ENDSEC                                    (End BLOCKS Section)
   0                                      (Begin ENTITIES Section)
SECTION
   2
ENTITIES
         (drawing entities go here)
   0
ENDSEC                                    (End ENTITIES Section)
   0
EOF                                       (End of File)
```

Learning Assignment 12

File management

This Assignment deals with the need to create and maintain

records of drawing files and
a back-up system for those files.

Early IT enthusiasts often claimed that computers would create the paperless office but a computer can easily generate such large quantities of paper-based data that this may become a problem.

In the drawing office, efficient use of CAD systems can reduce the amount of such data but it would be foolish to rely entirely on the computer system for all record-keeping.

A company must have a paper-based recording system for CAD drawings. There are advantages in using an extended version of a pre-CAD system. For example, pre-CAD staff are already familiar with it, and it will contain much of the information that the organisation needs; moreover, non-CAD staff may use it and it can be introduced quickly and easily.

A DBMS can print extensive data when a new design is completed. Such data can be used to expand the contents of manually kept files when required.

Task 12.1 File management

Note for supervisor   The trainees should each be given three floppy discs, with blank labels. Each disc is part of a 'grandfather, father, son' set and contains a drawing file representing one of three different stages in the creation of an incomplete CAD drawing. They should also be given a paper-based design which contains all the data required to complete the CAD version of the drawing.

There should be no *textual* information on the disc files, such as date, issue or modification number, to indicate the order in which they were created.

The trainees should be told that the completed design that was on the hard disc has been lost and needs to be re-created using the three discs and the paper-based design.

- Using your knowledge of the 'grandfather, father, son' system of back-up files, put the three discs into order.
- Number the discs to indicate the correct order of use.
- Using the information on the paper-based design and the appropriate disc data, complete the CAD design.
- Back-up the complete design on the appropriate disc.
- Complete a label for each disc.
- Compile a suitable written record of the design data and the disc details and give all your work to the supervisor.

Learning Assignment 13

Basic peripheral devices

This Assignment deals with the types of peripheral, or input and output, devices that are found on most CAD systems. When CAD is used for very specific applications, special input or output devices may be used but these are not dealt with here.

No peripheral device can be used by itself – it must be connected to a processing unit, sometimes called a computing unit. The notes at the end of Task 14.2 give more details.

The processing unit works with a keyboard, for input, and a display, or graphics, monitor for output. In addition, as you will know by now, using CAD efficiently requires a digitiser for input and a unit for producing a hard copy output or drawing.

Digitisers

Probably the most common CAD input device is a mouse but light pens, joysticks and graphics tablets can be used in a similar way to a mouse.

A graphics tablet, with either a puck or a stylus, is particularly useful when used as a digitiser, as this allows existing paper-based designs to be transferred to a CAD system. This is because the puck's crosshairs, or the point of the stylus, can be placed accurately at a given point, such as the intersection of two lines or the centre of a circle.

The drawing is attached to the tablet, usually by taping, and the entity type (line, circle, etc.) input so that the system can store the data correctly.

When the puck or stylus is correctly positioned, the pick button is pressed to transmit position data from the paper to the system. Finally, the end of the line or a point on the circle is picked to complete the input for that entity.

The companion core book of this series deals with input devices in greater detail.

Plotters

The majority of CAD users, whether in commerce or training organisations, will use an incremental, or X–Y, pen plotter for hard copy output. The alternative dot-matrix printer also gives good-quality text, but the graphics quality of a plotter is much better and plots can be on larger sheets.

The maximum size of sheet on standard dot-matrix printers is about 330 mm. Sheet sizes on standard flat-bed incremental plotters range from A4 up to A0, but a drum plotter, using a roll of paper rather than cut sheets, can produce larger drawings. Some drum plotters can also accept cut sheets.

As mentioned in Assignment 3, the CAD system needs to know about the output unit that is being used so that the special driver software of the CAD system can send the printing/plotting output instructions correctly. The more advanced CAD systems will provide a comprehensive menu of printer/plotter models to choose from.

Additional information

Because of the high cost of large good-quality plotters, and because the time taken to create a design far exceeds the time taken to output that design, it is normal practice for a plotter to be shared among several CAD designers. If the CAD systems are stand-alone, a switch box is used to select which system is connected to the plotter at a particular time. On a networked system, special software takes care of this problem.

More details about the relative merits of printers and plotters are given in the companion core book of this series.

Task 13.1 Plotting parameters

When a drawing is to be printed or plotted, it is usual for the CAD system screen to show a series of default parameters that can be altered before output starts. These will include sheet size, pen width (for plotters), pen colours, orientation, hidden line removal, drawing scale, design area to be plotted and so on.

Using the 'print screen' facility of your computer, obtain a printout of the variable plotting parameters of your CAD system. Find out, using the reference manual if necessary, the default values of the parameters and whether these agree with those given on the screen. If they are different, you should find out if they have been changed to suit company policy on plotted output before making any changes for your own plotting tasks.

Comparing costs

Because of the variation in hard copy production methods, there will be variation in hard copy costs. As well as paper size and quality variations, the cost of other consumable items will depend on the type of hard copy unit.

On dot-matrix printers, the life of printer ribbons will be reduced when dense hatching or thick lines are plotted. On plotters, the pen quality and cost vary widely: some plotters use ball-point pens, some use fibre-tip pens, and plotters at the top of the quality range use ceramic-tipped pens. Some automatic colour selection plotters use pens with coded barrels.

The special high-gloss plotting paper is expensive but is justified for quality plotting. On electrostatic and ink-jet plotters, special paper or film is normally used.

Task 13.2 Plotting designs

Note for supervisors Any of the drawings that have been produced by the trainee and that satisfy local training requirements can be used for this task. Only one plotting task is detailed but it should be repeated for each of the following requirements:

a scale of 1 to 1
a scale of 1 to 2
rotated by 90°
two at a scale of 1 to 2, side by side.

It is assumed that an A3 colour plotter is available.

- Load the drawing to be plotted from the floppy disc into the CAD system.
- Examine the drawing and note what colours are used in the layers that are to be plotted.
- Load the plotter with pens of the correct colour.
- Load the plotter with the correct size of paper.
- Set the plotting parameters such as origin, paper size, pen size, plot orientation, plot scale and so on.
- Produce a plot of the drawing. If the plot is incorrect in any way, repeat the necessary steps until a satisfactory plot is obtained.
- Make a note of any procedural item that would be of value when making future plots.

Learning Assignment 14

System performance and evaluation

This Assignment deals with the need to have a CAD system that performs at maximum efficiency at all times.

It is unlikely that you will be using CAD on a computer system that does not have a hard disc; this is because of the very large amount of fast-access memory that commercial CAD systems need.

Various methods, using special software, exist for efficient hard disc management but a treatment of these is beyond the scope of this workbook.

Your hard disc will perform better when all non-current design files have been removed. Archive them first, of course! Removing such files may not be the only way to improve disc performance, however – other factors are involved.

You may have enough computing ability to feel confident about working in the computer's operating system. You can then try to improve its performance by changing the directory structure or removing partially deleted files. If you are not sure, leave this type of work to someone who has more than an elementary computing knowledge.

If the CAD system is installed by the CAD supplier, you should find that it is set up to work efficiently. But computer system retailers cannot be experts on every computer applications package and, because of this, CAD packages may only be available through certain authorised suppliers.

If the computer and CAD software were not bought at the same time, you may find that the CAD system does not work very fast. In such cases, there may be a limit to what can be done to increase speed.

A speeding-up may be obtained if an additional co-processor circuit is fitted to carry out the large amount of calculation required for activities such as hatching, zooming or hiding. Fitting such a circuit may not improve the speed of a basic CAD system but some systems will not work without one.

Additional information

The cheapest CAD system to meet existing needs may be unable to satisfy new requirements that are identified after a few months operation. Ensure that the CAD system and the computer system can be upgraded – do not buy 'end-of-line' bargains that cannot be serviced or supported when problems occur.

Unless there is an electronics maintenance facility in the organisation, make certain that an on-site service agreement is included in the computer purchase price. There is no value in increasing productivity if you then have to wait for weeks to have the computer repaired.

Finally, when the CAD system is installed, there will have to be a period of time for staff training and familiarisation – as described earlier, system performance is also linked to the customisation of the CAD system. This cannot take place until the users have had several weeks, or even months, of experience with it.

Task 14.1 System capacity

Either by using the system manuals or by asking your supervisor, find out what hard disc capacity, RAM capacity, processor speed and floppy disc capacity your system has.

Task 14.2 System performance and evaluation

Note to supervisors   This task must be based on the hardware and software that is available to the trainee. Because these items will vary widely, a specific set of tasks is not provided.

A scenario of a possible CAD situation is given and, to guide trainees in the completion of the task, a framework on which to formulate answers is provided.

Read the following scenario of an imaginary CAD situation.

A 2D CAD system with wire-frame facilities is being used on a computer of the PC type fitted with a 4MHz processor but no maths co-processor.

The CAD software will run with or without a maths co-processor, and visual output is to a ten-inch monochrome screen monitor. The software cannot be configured to work with a digitiser and so all position input is via the cursor, or arrow, keys on the keyboard. The design data is stored on floppy disc using a $5\frac{1}{4}$-inch floppy disc drive.

A 20MB hard disc is fitted but is used only for the CAD system software and a wordprocessor package. A nine-pin dot-matrix printer is used mainly for printing wordprocessor documents but it is also used for printing A4-size drawings as CAD output.

The company produces specialised machines for folding and gluing cardboard containers of various sizes used, for example, by mail-order companies. The CAD system is used for the design of the many different sizes of glue nozzle that are used to meet the varying delivery requirements for glue. It was installed and configured some years ago by the company's draughtsman, who is due to retire shortly.

The CAD system is now being used, on a shared basis, by the draughtswoman who will take over from the draughtsman when he retires. As well as being computer-literate, she has followed, and qualified on, a one-year college course in the use of a commercial CAD system for engineering design.

She has spoken to the draughtsman about what she considers to be the limitations of the CAD system and its computer, and has suggested improvements that would, she is certain, improve design efficiency.

She admits that, even after using the system for six months, she cannot produce nozzle designs in the same time as the draughtsman even though, like her, he designs each new nozzle requirement from scratch.

She is convinced that in the nozzle drawing files that he has created over the previous twenty-five years there must be numerous examples of actual, or near, duplication of designs.

You are asked to draw up a proposal that will overcome the reservations given in the scenario concerning the overall usage efficiency of the CAD system. The proposal should not be restricted to a consideration of the CAD hardware and software.

The following comments should be used in drawing up the proposal:

1 A maths co-processor, when fitted, may affect the speed of features like zooming, hatching and regeneration.
2 Colour monitors are required if layers are to be used. Some CAD designs do not need layers and monochrome displays are widely used for wordprocessing.
3 Wordprocessing software normally uses the cursor (arrow) keys to select different parts of the document, but there are advantages in using a mouse for cursor control. It may be difficult to make a good case for using a digitising tablet for wordprocessing. Consider the possibility of a similar sort of argument for the CAD situation.
4 Although floppy discs are widely used for back-up purposes, their use during the design process may cause problems including a long access time when compared with a hard disc. A hard disc is almost certain to be used for the CAD software and you should consider whether there is a case for using it to hold current designs.

5 A 9-pin dot-matrix printer cannot compete with the 24-pin version for textual and graphics output quality. You may also consider that an A4 monochrome laser printer is justified.

6 In the scenario, the many nozzle designs differ only in dimensions and not in purpose or shape. Perhaps a case could be argued for a parametric design feature.

7 You might argue for a design database but any creation proposal should consider the merits or otherwise of a database for new designs only or one which includes existing designs.

Glossary

Bus   A term used to indicate that a peripheral device is connected to the computer using, usually, eight separate wires. This means that eight separate electrical signals can be conveyed at the same time, or in parallel. See also 'serial'.

Co-processor (maths)   An integrated circuit that deals with the many calculations that are required in a CAD system in order to increase the operating speed of the computer system.

Digitiser   A peripheral device that is used in a CAD system to input information about the screen position of the pointing symbol.

Display   The main computer output device that is similar to a television set.

Floppy disc   A thin circular piece of plastic that can be magnetised to hold computer information. The original versions were housed in square flexible plastic sleeves and were available in two sizes. The current version is smaller, holds more information and is housed in a stiff plastic sleeve.

Graphics monitor   A computer display unit with the high screen resolution necessary for the fine detail required on some CAD systems.

Hard disc parking   To prevent corruption of the information stored on the hard disc when the system was switched off, early versions required the read/write heads to be placed in a special position, or 'parked', on the disc surface.

KByte (KB)   A byte is a computer-based measuring unit that corresponds to one alphabetic character, and 1 KByte is about 1000 of these units. The capital, or upper case, 'K' is used because the exact value is 1024 rather than 1000 for which the small, or lower case, 'k' should be used.

Magnetic tape   A computer storage medium used mainly for back-up or archival purposes. It may be on a large reel or on smaller units similar to audio cassettes. Access to the stored information is much slower than when using floppy or hard discs.

MByte (MB)   This is approximately 1 million bytes – 1024 KBytes, to be exact.

MHz   An electrical frequency measuring unit meaning 1 million oscillations per second. In computer systems, it is used as a measure of the operating speed of the integrated circuits.

Monitor   An alternative term for a computer display unit.

Mouse   A computer input device that allows rapid positioning of the screen pointing symbol.

Networked system   An arrangement of interconnected computer systems that allows the sharing of expensive peripheral devices such as plotters and fast-access, high-capacity storage units.

Parameter   A limit or finite value defining or controlling the operational range of a CAD system function.

Processor   The main integrated circuit of a computer system. The term 'processor unit' is usually used to mean the complete arrangement of integrated circuits, power supply, interconnections, etc.

Puck   This is used in a similar way to a mouse but in conjunction with a special input device called a digitising tablet.

RAM   A term used to describe the main, very-fast-access storage unit of a computer system. Unlike other computer storage methods in use, the stored information is lost when the power supply is removed.

Serial   A term used to describe the connection method of some peripheral devices. The electrical signals are conveyed one after the other and this is a much slower method than the alternative 'bus' or parallel system.

Software   The set of computer operating programs for a particular application such as CAD.

Index